CABINET OF CURIOSITY

JAMES HANDSCOMBE

Together we unlock every learner's unique potential

At Hachette Learning (formerly Hodder Education), there's one thing we're certain about. No two students learn the same way. That's why our approach to teaching begins by recognising the needs of individuals first.

Our mission is to allow every learner to fulfil their unique potential by empowering those who teach them. From our expert teaching and learning resources to our digital educational tools that make learning easier and more accessible for all, we provide solutions designed to maximise the impact of learning for every teacher, parent and student.

Aligned to our parent company, Hachette Livre, founded in 1826, we pride ourselves on being a learning solutions provider with a global footprint.

www.hachettelearning.com

Although every effort has been made to ensure that website addresses are correct at time of going to press, Hachette Learning cannot be held responsible for the content of any website mentioned in this book. It is sometimes possible to find a relocated web page by typing in the address of the home page for a website in the URL window of your browser.

Hachette UK's policy is to use papers that are natural, renewable and recyclable products and made from wood grown in well-managed forests and other controlled sources. The logging and manufacturing processes are expected to conform to the environmental regulations of the country of origin.

To order, please visit www.HachetteLearning.com or contact Customer Service at education@hachette.co.uk / +44 (0)1235 827827.

ISBN: 978 1 0360 1347 9

© James Handscombe 2025

First published in 2025 by
Hachette Learning (a trading division of Hodder & Stoughton Limited),
An Hachette UK Company
Carmelite House
50 Victoria Embankment
London EC4Y 0DZ
www.HachetteLearning.com

The authorised representative in the EEA is Hachette Ireland, 8 Castlecourt Centre, Dublin 15, D15 XTP3, Ireland (email: info@hbgi.ie)

Impression number   10 9 8 7 6 5 4 3 2 1
Year   2029 2028 2027 2026 2025

All rights reserved. Apart from any use permitted under UK copyright law, no part of this publication may be reproduced or transmitted in any form or by any means, electronic or mechanical, including photocopying and recording, or held within any information storage and retrieval system, without permission in writing from the publisher or under licence from the Copyright Licensing Agency Limited. Further details of such licences (for reprographic reproduction) may be obtained from the Copyright Licensing Agency Limited, www.cla.co.uk

Typeset in the UK.

Printed and bound by CPI Group (UK) Ltd, Croydon, CR0 4YY

A catalogue record for this title is available from the British Library.

MIX
Paper | Supporting responsible forestry
FSC™ C104740

Acknowledgements

Saturday Live on BBC Radio 4, and rather obviously on Saturdays, has a regular feature called 'Inheritance Tracks' which teaches us that life is what happens somewhere between receiving from those who went before and passing on to those who come behind. On that basis I'd like to start by thanking all those who have fed my curiosity: teachers, tutors, parents and grandparents, I'd have a lot less to say if it weren't for you.

Similarly, I must thank all those students who have joined me in Cabinet of Curiosity classes. Thank you for the questions, suggestions, opinions and challenge – and particular thanks to those who recognise themselves in one of the anecdotes: you have made my life more interesting.

I'm grateful to both Harris Westminster and Harris Clapham Sixth Forms for providing both the amazing students to fill the classes and the flexibility of timetable that has allowed me the freedom to experiment.

Thank you to Andrew and Colin for reading early chapters and providing wise feedback on the direction and accuracy of my thinking.

Thank you to David for unexpectedly volunteering to read through and for being hugely generous with both time and red ink.

Particular thanks to my father, Rob, who read an early draft of the whole thing and helped me turn a jumble of potentially fascinating ideas into something coherent and potentially book-shaped.

Thanks also to the team at Hachette who have helped me take this idea from conception to physical book. Particular thanks to my editor, Elizabeth, who has corrected my errant punctuation, silently rephrased some of my more glaring verbal tics and suggested clarification when my turn for the elliptic has strayed into obfuscation and confusion.

Thanks, most of all, to Louisa, without whom everything I do would be worse and very little would be done at all.

James Handscombe was educated at Silverdale School in Sheffield, after which he earned a first in mathematics at Oxford University and a master's from Harvard. Since qualifying as a teacher he has worked in schools in South Wales, Australia and London. In 2014, he was appointed founding principal of Harris Westminster Sixth Form and since 2022 has been Executive Principal of both Harris Westminster and Harris Clapham Sixth Form.

His book *A School Built on Ethos* told the story of setting up Harris Westminster and explained how its success was built on the shared idea that learning is amazing. In *Cabinet of Curiosity* he unpicks the power of inquisitiveness.

To the next generation: two daughters, two nieces and six nephews.

Contents

Introduction: Curiosity is a superpower 1

Chapter 1: Culture and curiosity (Or what you need to know before you start) 5

Chapter 2: Topology (Or how to head into the unknown with a degree of confidence) 11

Chapter 3: The Palaeolithic era (Or how to fit three million years into 40 minutes) 21

Chapter 4: British politics 1979–1997 (Or the freedom of idiosyncrasy) 30

Chapter 5: Art appreciation for beginners (Or why interactivity beats lectures every time) 41

Chapter 6: *The Second Coming* by W.B. Yeats (Or why you can start with what you know but can't stay there) 47

Chapter 7: Quantum chromodynamics (Or how to bite off more than you can chew and not choke) 54

Chapter 8: American politics, history and government (Or the joy of reacting to current affairs) 63

Chapter 9: A collection of miscellanea (Or the joy of having choices) 76

Chapter 10: Throwing open to the floor (Or how I stopped worrying and learned to love the unknown) 89

Chapter 11: The curiosity toolkit (Or what I've learned from 20 cohorts and two schools) 97

Appendix: How I delivered the sessions – notes for teachers 106

Bibliography 119

Introduction
Curiosity is a superpower

This is a story about a step into the unknown, a metaphorical journey of the mind that took me from having an idea about curiosity to teaching students how to be more curious. Because I don't like to underuse a good metaphor, it's also about how the experience of curiosity involves a step into the unknown – an analogy that allows us to interrogate the unknown, to find out what kind of territory asking questions takes us into. We'll get more detail later, but for now let's establish that the unknown is not the empty void of outer space: there is, as *The X-Files* tells us, something out there. Nor does it have to be a wilderness into which our half-fledged things are set free: part of my goal was to be able to play the wise guide. I think the unknown is more like a wonderful and labyrinthine library with surprises round every corner. The step into the unknown is hard because there's no way of knowing what kind of unknown you face, but once in the labyrinth you lose that fear – you still don't know what you'll find, but you can be sure that if you keep going you'll get to something worth looking for. The thing about curiosity, you see, is that one thing leads to another; answers lead to questions and questions lead to answers. But I get ahead of myself.

One thing leads to another. That statement, for example, could lead to a rumination on history by Toynbee or Rudge; it could be a statement of causality and be limited by the speed of light; it could inspire poets to write about how way leads onto way or to warn against stepping out on a road that goes ever on. In this case, it leads to a book – this book – which is about the way questions lead to answers and answers lead to questions, but which was itself the result of another book. Being unable to follow the advice of the King of Hearts and begin at the beginning, and yet having to begin somewhere, we take as our starting point that other book.

In 2017, I contributed to a collection of essays entitled *World Class: Tackling the Ten Biggest Challenges Facing Schools Today* (James and Warwick, 2017). In exchange for my words, I received a free copy of the book and took advantage of this serendipity to find out what others had thought and said. One chapter, by Claire Fox, focused on curiosity – the art of asking questions and expecting answers – and, reading it, I was convinced of the idea that *curiosity is a superpower*.

I refer to Claire in passing as if I know her. I don't, though I know of her: sometime Member of the European Parliament for North West England, keen on Brexit, admired by Boris Johnson and elevated to the House of Lords by him, where she sits as an unaffiliated peer despite a long-term objection to the unelected upper chamber. Earlier I referred to Toynbee and Rudge; I don't know either of them, not least because Toynbee is dead (before that he was Arnold J. Toynbee, professor of history at the London School of Economics and Political Science) and Rudge is fictional (he's one of Alan Bennett's 'history boys'). The King of Hearts is from *Alice's Adventures in Wonderland*, the poets I referred to earlier are J.R.R. Tolkien and Robert Frost, and Boris Johnson is the erstwhile prime minister whose place in this story is limited to this paragraph.

I digress. Let me retrace my steps through Boris Johnson, Claire Fox and essays on world-class schools to the two schools in which I've worked while I've been on my journey of curiosity. Harris Westminster Sixth Form (HWSF) has been around since 2014: it's located not far from Parliament Square in central London and attracts academically able students from all over the capital – with a particular focus on the most disadvantaged. Harris Clapham Sixth Form (HCL6F) is about half an hour further south in the Brixton/Clapham borderlands and, being a non-selective school for Lambeth students, serves a community that is narrower geographically but broader academically. The curiosity journey starts in Harris Westminster and is then transplanted to Harris Clapham – which has been an interesting exercise in seeing how the ideas survive in the real world, out of the somewhat Hogwartian environment of HWSF.

Reading Claire Fox's essay caused me to ruminate on the challenges of offering disadvantaged students a souped-up, turbo-charged academic education in the two years of sixth form. Some of them take to it like waterbirds to the Serpentine but others flounder and shrink into their shells. (I'm not entirely sure what kind of creature this metaphor compares teenagers with – some kind of web-footed flying snail?) The thought crystallised that some of the students who got least out of Harris

Westminster were missing out because they had not been taught to be curious. The rest of *World Class* was set aside as I disappeared into that rabbit hole, wondering what I could do to teach them to be curious.

An artist's impression of a typical student

Curiosity! Everybody knows that curiosity killed the cat but how many of us have looked more deeply to find out which cat? Lovers of the Elizabethan theatre will know that Ben Jonson (in 1598) and William Shakespeare (in 1599, as far as any of his work can be accurately dated) used this phrase (with 'curiosity' being replaced by 'care' but keeping the same meaning) and whether or not our feline friends were dying this way before that time, they have been, metaphorically at least, ever since. I am not the first to have the idea that *curiosity is a superpower*. In his book *Sapiens: A Brief History of Humankind* (2015), Yuval Noah Harari muses on the possibility that a key turning point in human development was when we moved from saying, 'There is a hill' to 'I wonder what is over that hill.' Many others have written or spoken on the subject. It is, however, a long-established and honourable habit of teachers to magpie ideas from wherever they can find them, picking them up, turning them over in their beaks (or minds) and wondering whether they can be applied to the business of education.

Back at Harris Westminster, we already had a school that encouraged and rewarded curiosity, where questions were indulged and answered from the teachers' extensive knowledge or via some out-of-class research. (Actually, indulged feels too weak a verb for a part of learning that exemplifies the nature of the school – we don't merely indulge questions: we rejoice in them, celebrate anyone who can answer them and dive enthusiastically into the opportunity for learning that unanswered questions represent.) We nurture geekiness both through our super-curriculum and extracurricular opportunities. The super-curriculum is our word for those bits of the education that aren't immediately directed at qualifications. Key to this book is the notion of Cultural Perspectives (CPs): these are lessons that take place twice a week in the Year 12 timetable and are term-long courses (about eight taught sessions plus some time for writing a 'response' – an assessed piece of work) that are chosen from a menu created from the enthusiasms of those teachers assigned to deliver them.

Students who arrived at Harris Westminster already curious found themselves in a sort of academic playground where a virtuous circle of questions and answers led them deeper into learning. My challenge was those who didn't see school in this way, who wanted to write the answers down and move on – who had been taught that this was the way to succeed and found the divergent alternative baffling.

So, what to do? This book attempts to explain what we did and maybe to encourage you, my readers (hello), to have a go. There are 11 chapters. Chapter 1 describes our programme of CPs and the module about curiosity that fits into it. The next seven chapters each take one of the sessions that might appear (as though from a cabinet) in that module – in each one I give a taste of the content and then reflect on why I think it deserves its place and how it fits in with our overall vision. More detailed notes for teachers who want to take on the challenge of delivering these sessions can be found in the appendix at the end of the book. The last three chapters gradually edge away from this format. Chapter 9 rattles through some topics that have sometimes made it onto the course but haven't, for one reason or another, been awarded their own chapter; chapter 10 talks about a different structure for a kind of session that takes curiosity to the next level (one thing leading to another again) and chapter 11 is an overview, a conclusion and my best attempt to distil the meandering journey I've been on into a handful of enumerated signposts.

Chapter 1
Culture and curiosity (Or what you need to know before you start)

My hypothesis is that those students who arrive at school lacking curiosity are at a disadvantage because *curiosity is a superpower*. The more curious you are, the more questions you ask, the more answers you get, the more you know and also the more curious and questioning you become. The pay-off comes in the knowledge that is acquired, knowledge that in the most transactional way translates into exam grades but which has far wider applicability. But the key miracle comes in that virtuous circle.

Unfortunately, schools, qualifications and curricula are not always set up to encourage curiosity and often do send the message that the point is to write the correct answers down and leave interesting questions alone. I put my mind to remedying this deficiency. I said to myself: if the problem is they have learned not to be curious, then they simply need to learn the opposite, and so, being a schoolteacher, I just need to put them into a classroom where I teach curiosity. But where would it fit during the school day? For us at Harris Westminster (and later at Harris Clapham), the answer was straightforward. We would fit it into our already established Cultural Perspectives (CPs) programme.

The idea behind CPs is that interesting conversations are worth having and that interesting conversations occur when one person knows something the other doesn't but is interested in. I say 'worth having', and I believe it's true, but that worth is difficult to pin down – it's unlikely that knowing a bit about Greek myths will help you get a job, and even less likely that an appreciation of classical music will get you through your maths A-level. What we're talking about here is cultural capital – which is a fraught phrase because of the question of which cultures represent capital. My definition is that 'cultural capital' is learning that facilitates communication and understanding between groups of people. This includes literature, such as the Greek myths, because of the power of a reference to a shared story, but is perhaps best exemplified in the five great mathematical jokes (this is a collective name that so far only I use, but which I remain convinced will catch on). The first of these is simply: 'What is sinx over n?' and the answer is '6, because the ns cancel.'

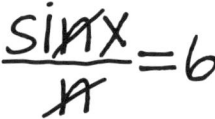

A great mathematical joke

This is obviously mathematical and has the structure of a joke, but is great – to my mind at least – because it relies on the audience sharing some knowledge: to find this funny you need to know that fractions can be cancelled down by finding a common factor, but you also need to know that you can't do this with the n in sinx because sin is a function rather than the product of s, i and n. I'm reliably informed that if you have to explain why a joke is funny then it isn't and so I shall leave the other four to tantalise the reader along with the story of Tantalus.

CPs are thus lessons in things that the teacher thinks are worth knowing but which don't come up in either examined courses or compulsory PSHE (personal, social, health and economic education – the catch-all phrase for such things as sex education and warnings against the evils of drugs). We take CPs very seriously: teachers have to prepare schemes of work with plans for the eight lessons and write titles and teasers that are published for students to help them select from the list. The courses finish with a piece of assessed work and grades are reported to parents. We take them seriously because students listen to what their teachers say, and if they are told, or maybe just infer, that non-qualification learning is less important than their A-levels then they will ignore it, truant lessons, mess around in class and avoid doing their assignments. They'll do this not because they are naughty, but because they think that's the right thing to do, that they *should* be concentrating on their examined courses. We know that qualifications are important, both because they represent a quantity of learning and because they are a transferrable measure of those skills and knowledge, but we think it is the learning itself that is the critical thing and that teachers have a responsibility to encourage rather than restrict it. We argue that learning is amazing and that any syllabus is inevitably constrained and limited and, as a consequence, must be a poor reflection on the wonders of the universe.

When we created our curriculum to include compulsory CP lessons, the fear was that students would decide that CPs were less important than 'real subjects' and passively neglect them; and the natural response to this fear would have been to equivocate, to give ground on this fight so as not to undermine the other studies we're encouraging. The reason that we've made them work is that we've shunned this natural response in favour of a wholehearted commitment that says that CPs are the best part of the week, that they are an opportunity for students to learn what might otherwise have passed them by, and for teachers to share their enthusiasms and passions with a willing (or, at least, captive) audience. One of the key truths of education is that good kids will do things for marks – and that most students are 'good kids', that they actually want to do the right thing, to please the adults in their lives (most of the time). So the response of most students to our wholehearted commitment, our awarding of marks and our reporting to parents has been enthusiastic engagement and therefore enjoyment of what might otherwise have been a drag.

So, with a CP programme in play and the freedom of all teachers to pitch for a new module on it, all I had to do was come up with my own module. To be fair, 'all' is doing some heavy lifting in that last sentence, but the idea that I landed on was that I could try to do three things:

1 **Model curiosity** – be interested in things that I really had no right to be interested in; be visibly fascinated by chunks of knowledge from all areas of thought.

2 **Inspire curiosity** – tell stories, explain ideas, structure knowledge in a way that makes knowing about whatever it is attractive; that leaves students thinking that perhaps they would like to know more about this topic even though it is new to them and not 'the right answer' to any question they would foreseeably be asked.

3 **Expect curiosity** – explicitly demand questions, thoughts and responses in unfamiliar situations; tell students to be curious; give my *'curiosity is a superpower'* talk and have them respond to whatever I show them with some curiosity of their own.

And so, over the next month or so I pieced these ideas together into an eight-week CPs course. Each week I would stand up and present a body of knowledge from a different area of study using my imagination, wit and teaching experience to make it accessible and interesting. The conceit was that I would be drawing my talks from a 'cabinet of curiosity' with the style of a Renaissance scholar showing off new specimens looted on his latest expedition (but without the actual despoiling of treasures). Students would be encouraged to ask questions and if I didn't know the answer (which seemed quite likely given I was going to stray a long way from my comfort zone) then we could both delight in trying to find out the answers in the intervening week.

It would be unidiomatic at this point not to explore the idea of the Renaissance cabinet of curiosity, although I should confess that I knew little of this when I started out – the cabinet was a picture rather than a history lesson (the picture in question being by Domenico Remps and from the 1690s). A 'cabinet' was a room that would be filled with an encyclopaedic collection of objects – from natural history, geology, ethnography and archaeology. It formed a basis for enquiry, for categorisation and for imagination (the narwhal horn was a staple of such cabinets, often mistakenly or mischievously attributed to a unicorn). It was also a status symbol through which the wealthy collector could demonstrate their good taste and scholarship.

So, back to my module. I made a list of school subjects and topics within them about which I had ideas or questions that, if I was to examine further, might, with some work, turn into something interesting to other people. The first two or three leaped neatly onto the page, but before I reached number eight, and the end of my list, I began to realise that I was going to be attempting something quite difficult. Unfortunately for me, I'd already spoken to colleagues about this idea and, with a glorious display of confidence, they had told me they thought it was great and I should definitely do it (while visibly making a mental note not to undertake such a task themselves). I couldn't face accepting that I'd bitten off a larger academic challenge than I could comfortably chew and so returned to my list and started to put together a collection of slides on which to base my talks.

This book explores some of that activity and the hope in writing it is not only to encourage curiosity in the reader but also to equip them (you) to share curiosity with others, particularly if you happen to be in the fortunate position of working in a school. Philip Larkin tells us that church is the place to go in order to grow more serious – I've developed the cabinet to be a place where we can grow more curious. I hope that you, dear reader, will find your curiosity rewarded in this book and that some of you (mostly, I imagine, those of you who are teachers) will be inspired to build and share your own collection. Your cabinet will, I'm sure, contain different wonders from mine, but I hope there will be enough ideas here that you're not short of possibilities and even if you decide not to teach a topic yourself, I hope to pique your curiosity and leave you wanting to know more about some things that you hadn't previously considered.

Leaping to the far end of the process and looking back on seven years of Cabinets, I feel confident that they have had a positive impact on the students who have attended them: I wouldn't claim to have single-handedly solved the curiosity deficit, but there are very few who haven't come out more interested in things than they went in. For some of them this has been stepping off from ground zero (absolutely hating the idea of being in a room of curiosity) to accepting that, given they had to write about something they found interesting (and the final stage of the course is to do exactly that), there were some things they found interesting enough to write about. Others have come in already fascinated by the world and asking questions and they have been delighted to find kindred spirits and to have their attention pointed towards areas that had never struck them as being worthy of study. There have also been those who have exemplified my original goal, who joined the course vaguely positive but not sure what to expect and who learned what being curious looks like, who developed their skills of listening and thinking and asking good questions. The most rewarding outcome for me has probably come from those students whose final reflection read something like this: 'I know I haven't contributed as much to the course as others and that I have probably not got as much out of it as I could, but I have really enjoyed learning about <insert whichever topic sparked their imagination – often to my personal surprise> and will endeavour in any future classes to ask more questions and volunteer more opinions.'

I've now opened the Cabinet of Curiosity to close to 20 groups (which has vindicated my decision to put my planning onto slides – something I only rarely do when teaching my subject (maths) but which has enabled me to remember both content and structure accurately in areas where, deliberately and knowingly, I'm teaching things I know far less about). These groups span two schools and while Harris Westminster Sixth Form has an otherworldly air that comes both from a selective intake and a location on Parliament Square, our set-up at Harris Clapham Sixth Form may be more relatable: we have a broad entry, a mixed curriculum of A-levels and general vocational courses, and a location that brings one firmly back to earth in South London. I sincerely hope that teachers reading this are inspired and equipped to give something similar a go, that leaders are convinced that the curriculum time is worth the investment (it absolutely is – students armed with curiosity superpowers do better and are more fun in other lessons), and that any students who have ventured thus far are able to enjoy the meanderings of an old teacher and to share with me a delight in all things curious.

One final point. Pick up any play – Shakespeare, Beckett, Stoppard – and read the script. Now go and see that play. The difference between the page and the stage is remarkable and mirrored by the challenge of presenting three-dimensional and interactive lessons in a book. Unfortunately, I can't invite you all into my sessions but I have done my best with the following chapters to hint at the energy, fun and bounce that takes place, and yes, most of all, the learning of how to be curious. The other difference between the performed play and the script is that on stage you can make mistakes, get your words wrong and commit dreadful anachronisms without fear: few of the audience will notice, few of those who do will comment, and those that do both will be so deeply committed as to make the engagement a delight. My greatest fear in turning my performances into a book is that I will appear to be posing as an authority on areas of knowledge where I'm really not – and will attract condemnation for my inevitable errors. Let me prepare you by saying that everything in this book is true to the limits of my understanding and that I've done rather more research than would be expected of a teacher going beyond their subject but that it's not an academic treatise – in most areas of intellectual endeavour I'm an enthusiastic amateur rather than an expert.

Chapter 2
Topology
(Or how to head into the unknown with a degree of confidence)

It is said among the wise that you should at least start with what you know even if you don't intend to stay there, and if you are going to lecture then you should choose something you can present with clarity, confidence and enthusiasm.

This presents me with a difficulty. My home turf is mathematics and no one in their right mind would start with maths, right? Actually, including maths at all has to be a no-no in most people's lists but mathematics won my heart long ago and so maths it is. I have two things in my favour. First, my initial attempt at this module was to Harris Westminster students, who are a clever and keen bunch, and second, I am forewarned. I have met non-mathematicians: I know I have to slow down and keep it as interactive as possible.

We start by drawing a network – a sort of simplified map with faces (that take the place of countries), edges (borders) and vertices (places borders meet or intersect).

Cabinet of Curiosity

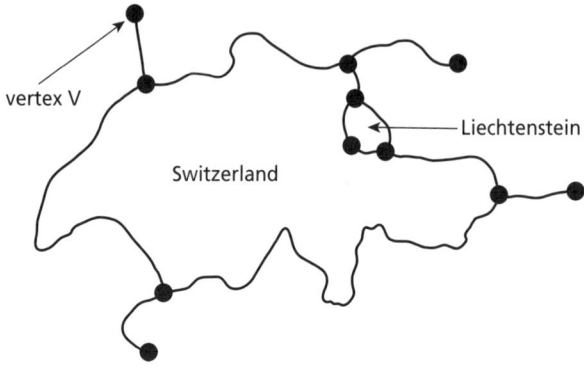

Switzerland

This simplified map of Switzerland is a network and illustrates the rules of networks, which are as follows:

1. There must be at least one vertex.
2. Each vertex must be reachable from every other vertex following the edges.
3. Every edge joins two vertices. This means vertex V (see diagram) is crucial – without it the edge wouldn't obey this rule. In networks, you are not allowed to leave an edge dangling.
4. No two edges cross.
5. A face is surrounded by edges.
6. A face must be in one piece (topologists say 'connected') – you have to be able to walk from any point in a face to any other point without leaving the face.
7. A face cannot have any holes in it – if you tie one end of a ball of string to a lamppost and go for a walk inside the face, letting out the string as you go until you get back to the lamppost, then you have to be able to pull the string back in without the string leaving the face.

You may be looking at the network and asking one or both of the following questions:

- Why is the map called 'Switzerland' when one of the two faces clearly represents Liechtenstein?
- How come Liechtenstein has three vertices – surely one of these is redundant?

The answers are:

- That was an oversight; from now on I shall call this entity Switzenstein.
- It's absolutely fine to have 'redundant' vertices, edges or faces – the network is a mathematical construction and these elements don't mathematically mean anything, they just are. The third vertex on Liechtenstein is there simply because it pleased me aesthetically (and to make this point – thank you for asking the question).

A simplified map of Italy will demonstrate how one could draw something that wasn't a network:

Italy

The problems here (mathematically, I make no comment on geopolitics – at least not in this session) are the Vatican City and San Marino. As drawn, we are breaking rules 2, 3 and 7.

Rule 2: Each vertex must be reachable from every other vertex – here the San Marino vertex is not.

Rule 3: Every edge joins two vertices – here, the Vatican City edge joins no vertices. The San Marino edge, by the way, is fine – you can have an edge joining a vertex to itself.

Rule 7: A face cannot have any holes in it – here, the Italy face has two holes (one for the Vatican City and one for San Marino). If you walked all the way round one of the smaller faces trailing string behind you to make a loop, then you couldn't pull the loop in without it leaving Italy.

We can make this into a network (which, following precedent, I shall call 'San Italican') by adding a vertex and two edges. Notice that Italy is still a single face because you can wander across it without crossing any edges. (We don't care about having to do a really huge road trip for these purposes.)

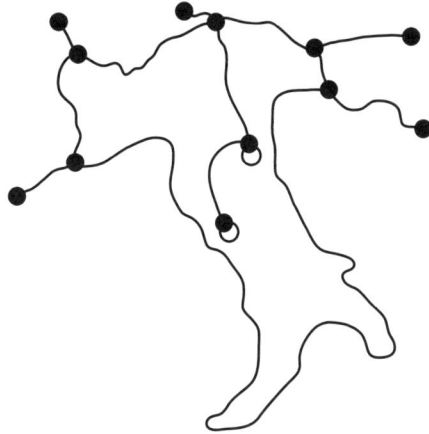

San Italican

We can now, and you would have thought this would be quite straightforward but experience says otherwise, count the number of vertices, edges and faces in our networks and put them in a table.

Network	Vertices	Edges	Faces
Switzenstein	11	12	2
San Italican	12	14	3

Because I have only two networks it's unlikely that you'll see a pattern, but there is one and you can experiment with a pen and some paper to try to find it. I recommend drawing smaller networks with just a handful of vertices for ease of counting and will wait here until you're done.

Ok. We can add another column on the right with the formula $V - E + F$ and note that $11 - 12 + 2$ (Switzenstein) and $12 - 14 + 3$ (San Italican) both give 1. If you have done your own experiment then you will find that all correctly drawn and counted networks give the same answer.

Why is this true? Good question. The kind of question we are here to celebrate. One version of the answer lies in a mathematical idea called induction, which tells us to start with very simple ideas and build our way upwards. From the definitions above, you can see that for something to be a network it has to have a vertex, but everything else is optional. The proof has four steps:

Step A   The simplest possible network has just one vertex, no edges and no faces: V − E + F is $1 − 0 + 0 = 1$.

Step B   Any network apart from the single vertex is built up from a simpler one by adding edges and vertices one at a time. When we're doing this we make sure that each step in our building obeys the rules of networks.

Step C   If you add edges and vertices legally then you don't change the V − E + F total. This is a key stage in our argument and at the moment there's no reason to believe it's true – I'll justify it in a minute but for now just hold onto this thought.

Step D   If V − E + F starts off at 1 and never changes then it will be 1 for any network you draw.

If each of these four statements is true then our conjecture – that every network has a V − E + F score of 1 – is mathematically proved. The tricky part of the proof is step C (we've checked A, B is obvious and D is a summary).

Proving Step C:

We claim that if we have a network and we add an edge or a vertex legally then we will not change the V − E + F score. A little thought tells us that there are only three legal ways to extend a network and so there are only three cases to check:

Case a)   Add a vertex in the middle of nowhere and join it to an existing vertex with an edge.

Case b)   Add a vertex in the middle of an existing edge.

Case c)   Add an edge joining two existing vertices (this includes adding an edge joining a single existing vertex to itself).

In case a), adding one vertex and one edge means adding one and subtracting one from our V − E + F total, keeping it the same.

In case b), adding a vertex and turning one edge into two edges again means we add one and subtract one.

In case c), it depends on whether the edge is on the outside of the network (see c(i) below) or if it goes across the middle of an existing face (see c(ii) below).

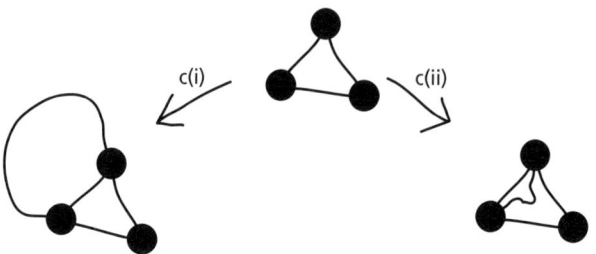

Two ways to add an edge

In c(i) we add an edge and a brand new face and in c(ii) we add an edge and split an existing face into two faces. In either case, both E and F increase by one so V – E + F remains the same.

This is an interesting curiosity, but the power of the idea comes when we draw networks on surfaces in three dimensions. If you're following along with a permanent marker, you can go and try this on a selection of household items (please ask permission from the owner first), but here we will look at five 'platonic solids', which are carefully defined regular polyhedra (solids formed by plane faces). The platonic solids are the tetrahedron, cube, octahedron, dodecahedron and icosahedron and are well known to players of Dungeons and Dragons for providing fair dice with increasing numbers of sides.

Object	Vertices	Edges	Faces	V – E + F
Tetrahedron	4	6	4	2
Cube	8	12	6	2
Octahedron	6	12	8	2
Dodecahedron	20	30	12	2
Icosahedron	12	30	20	2

There are two interesting things here. The first is that we get the same answer for V – E + F for each of these objects. The second is that we have a different answer for the surface of our 3D shapes than we did for the flat networks on the sheet of paper. Wow! Somehow this calculation encapsulates something about the surface we're drawing on.

That something becomes clearer if we draw on the surface of a doughnut – a ring one, rather than one filled with jam or custard (if you have bought such an item, I recommend eating it rather than drawing on it).

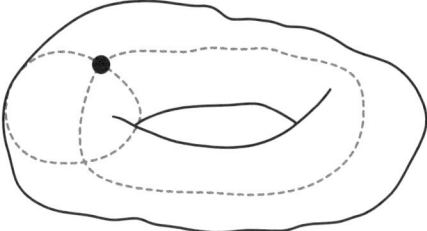

A doughnut network

The simplest network (shown above) now has one vertex, two edges and one face. It's possible that the visualisation is difficult, especially if you have just eaten your doughnut, so let me clarify. For our network to be legal we must have a vertex, so we draw one on. We're not done yet because we have broken rule 7 – there's a hole in our face. In fact, there are two ways we could set out with our ball of string and make a loop that we couldn't haul back in: we could walk round the hole in the doughnut or we could go for a loop through the hole, round the outside and back to where we started. In order to make this face legal we have to draw two edges essentially following those two routes (marked with dotted lines on the diagram). With those edges drawn in, we have a legal network and can calculate V − E + F = 1 − 2 + 1 = 0. If, on your experimentation with three-dimensional objects, you took your marker to something with a hole in it (or with a handle, such as a coffee mug), then you would have got 0 in your calculation. At the time, this would have been perplexing when all the other 3D objects were giving a score of 2, but should now have you saying, 'Wow!'

The key point here is that there is a lot about the shape that doesn't matter for the purposes of V − E + F: it can have sticky-outy bits, indentations, sharp corners and so on, but the only thing that matters is the hole – for this purpose all shapes with one hole are the same and all shapes with no holes are the same. (I'll wait while the eager beavers nip off to find something with two holes – maybe a two-handled drinking bowl.) Different branches of mathematics are distinguished by which objects they consider basically the same and which are considered different. In geometry, which is the way shapes are most often studied in school mathematics, there is an idea of congruence – two shapes are the same if you can move one so it fits exactly over the other without otherwise changing it. Whole lessons are spent on identifying exactly which characteristics of triangles you must have ascertained to be sure they are congruent. Even more simply, we know that two fractions are equivalent if you can cancel them down to the same number. Every branch of maths has its own definition and topology is the study of shapes that are the same if you can squidge or squish one shape into another as though it were made of rubber. (There is a proper mathematical formalisation of this but it's not going to help us much at this stage – the key point is that when it comes to ordinary objects such as you might find around the house, in a school classroom or, in fact, anywhere in our physical universe, the only aspect that topologists are interested in is the number of holes.)

With two holes in a shape we get $V - E + F = -2$. (If you found that two-handled drinking bowl, you'll be able to check this – if not, then you'll have to take my word for it). In general, we get the formula $V - E + F = 2 - 2H$, where H is the number of holes. Hang on, though! We started with a collection of networks where $V - E + F$ was 1, which doesn't make any sense at all unless there's half a hole in your sheet of paper. The resolution is that we haven't really covered the whole paper – there's an external 'face' that we haven't counted which takes us to a total of 2 and confirms that the globe we're drawing on is actually a sphere.

$V - E + F$ is called the Euler characteristic of the surface, named after Leonhard Euler, an amazingly prolific Swiss mathematician of the eighteenth century. The amazing thing, apart from having dipped a toe into the rabbit hole of advanced mathematics, is that something that seems so local, so mundane as drawing country borders, can somehow tell us something global about the shape of the world we're drawing on.

Rationale and reflections

The key property of any session I pull out of the Cabinet is that it should be interesting; that it should reward curiosity. Given that it is my thesis that there is an inexhaustible supply of such topics, I have had to use other criteria to select from the available cornucopia of curiosity. Sessions are not only justified by their individual merit but by how they fit with their neighbours: each one offers a different kind of curiosity, raises different questions, rewards different modes of thinking. Since this book is an examination of curiosity as well as a stimulus to it, we take a step back at the end of each chapter to think about why this idea deserves its place.

There are a few reasons why I like topology to be the first session, but the most important one is that maths is my subject and this is something I can speak confidently, authoritatively and passionately about which far outweighs the corresponding disadvantage of not modelling learning that is new to all of us when it comes to reeling students in, getting them onside and persuading them to travel with me – there will be time for me to leave my security blanket in future sessions. I would therefore recommend to anyone putting their own cabinet together (which I assume you will all do once you have finished reading and taking a permanent marker to household items) to start with your own subject and, within that, find something that you would love to add to the syllabus but that isn't there at the moment.

That might mean – as with my topic – that it's a little difficult, that there are moments of bafflement, and that there are definitely unanswered questions when the lesson comes to an end. Those unanswered questions are not defects – they are integral to the purpose of the course. If students go off wondering about platonic solids, what other stuff Euler came up with or even how this would all work in four dimensions, then they've picked up some curiosity already. Even if you're not a mathematician, then the window this activity opens onto the wide vistas of university mathematics could justify its place in your cabinet. It might be worth prepping the school librarian so that there are suitable books to which students can be directed (a bibliography can be found at the end of this book).

Another advantage of this session is that it has a practical activity – there's more student interaction in this one than in most others. This makes it more accessible and enables me to get to know the class a bit, and for them to relax a bit with me while they count and recount the features of their network.

The key point of the first session is to set out the stall – we're a class where asking questions is the most important thing; where there isn't a 'right answer' we've got to get to and where getting sidetracked can take us to interesting places. It's a class where all students are expected to engage – quietly avoiding eye-contact is not an option. The sooner this all becomes clear – particularly the participation and questioning element – the more likely it is that students will realise they should take part before they get to the end of the course. Taking part means asking questions and asking questions means being curious.

How hard do I have to work at getting the students to take part? The basic structure of the session ensures that most students easily throw themselves into it but, as ever, the importance of the class leader (me, in this case) putting in the work can vary depending on the students. When we've used the Cabinet as an entry-level CPs class for students who don't show much enthusiasm for learning, there have been several who have entered clearly determined not to be enchanted by my nonsense. One of these responded to the request to draw a network by doing absolutely nothing – at the time my definition of a network did not include rule 1, requiring the existence of at least one vertex. I'd not realised that this was necessary and his blank page was technically a legal submission. I made a big thing about this and his genius in spotting what I hadn't, added the rule specifying at least one vertex and then asked him to draw a network that satisfied all of the new rules. One vertex, a dot in the centre of the page, was his minimalistic response – it took quite a bit of time for me to win him round (meanwhile, I restructured my rules so that they covered all bases).

Final comment on this: if you have an enthusiasm, go for it. Make it the first session in your module. Realise, of course, that it might not be everyone's enthusiasm so take it slowly, make it practical, make it interactive. Make it fun. Give permission for errors. Make having a go more important than getting it right. Make sure you use the magic words, 'That's a great question.' The more often you use them now, when the answer is tucked up your sleeve, the less you'll feel like a fraud when you're off home turf and just don't know.

Chapter 3
The Palaeolithic era (Or how to fit three million years into 40 minutes)

Welcome to the Stone Age! Home to cavemen, woolly mammoths, scantily clad hunters, Neanderthals, fire, the wheel and, erm, probably not dinosaurs, which had been extinct for about 140 million years before our story starts, despite what the makers of *The Flintstones* would have you believe. The 'Stone Age' gets touched upon in primary school history lessons but doesn't often come up again at school – a structure that left me (and, if responses to this session are representative, a lot of other people) poorly informed and imagining that it covers a similar time period to the Bronze Age, Iron Age and Dark Ages. In order to examine this idea and to learn more about the Stone Age, we start with the fact that this is the beginning of human history and then have to wonder what the starting point for humanity might be. This question immediately throws us from history, through archaeology and into evolutionary biology with whiplash-inducing speed. We are used to the distinction between human and not-human being genetically, biologically clear but over the time span of the Stone Age there is a grey area – it quickly becomes clear that there is no 'starting point' for humanity, no moment in history before which there were no humans and after which there were humans. A better question is: 'What does it mean to be human?' The language to describe the transition from not-human through partially-human to human is also difficult (for one thing, I'm not going to be using the phrase partially-human any more) so, rather than terms such as 'animal' or, worse, 'creature', I'm going to use the technical term 'hominin', which covers the descendants of the last common ancestor of humans and chimpanzees.

'Hominid' would include all common ancestors of gorillas and orangutans as well, but we won't need to go that far back in our story – in fact, we won't be going all the way back to the human/chimpanzee split, but how far should we go to make sure we cover the development of the distinctive aspects of humanity? One conceivable answer to that question might be the first recorded use of tools, if we decide that extensive tool use is what sets humans apart from other animals. We don't really know how or when early wooden tools were used as these have rotted away (although our earliest evidence for tool use is fossilised animal bones that are marked by tools so it's not completely impossible to trace their existence even if we have no surviving specimens) and so we begin by looking for the earliest stone tools, the start of the Stone Age. At the time of writing, the earliest discovered tools we know of date from 3.3 million years ago (one key point for this session is that any idea of AD, CE, BC or BCE is made completely redundant by the timescale – we talk about years BP, before the present). These tools were found in East Africa and we don't know what species made them although the smart money, based on what skeletons have been found nearby, is probably on the genus *Australopithecus*.

Australopithecus was a collection of related species of hominins, human-like apes, or possibly ape-like humans, that lived in Africa between about four million and two million years BP. They had small brains (about a third of the size of humans'), were small (1.3 m tall) and walked bipedally. The first tools were made by taking largish stones from a riverbed and chipping flakes away from the core to make one or more sharp edges. These weren't weapons primarily, but were used for slicing meat from bones and bark from branches or roots, and for cracking open bones to get at the high-energy marrow inside. The largest collection of early stone tools is found at Olduvai Gorge in Tanzania where tools can be found from a span of about a million years and show a very slow development of technological sophistication.

In *A History of the World in 100 Objects* (2012), the director of the British Museum, Neil MacGregor, looks at one of these tools, made about 1.8 million years ago, and reflects on what it is that makes us think that the toolmaker was human. The key idea, maybe, is that of dissatisfaction – of wanting to make good things better: the tool could have been functional with two chips taken out of it, but we see one with eight – the result of a mind that thought, 'This would work better if I put some more effort into it.'

You will have noticed that the dates don't quite add up. Partly this is the result of a great deal being unknown, dates being approximate in the first place and rounded by me for simplicity; but partly this is because *Australopithecus* was replaced by *Homo habilis*, a sufficiently similar species but sufficiently poorly evidenced (just a handful of skeletons) that debate rages as to whether it should be classed as *Homo* at all, or as a continuation: *Australopithecus habilis*. This highlights one of the challenges, and delights, of this field of scholarship – we're making guesses on fragments of information that survive by chance from a huge span of years. There's so much more we might be able to find and so much scope for new findings to completely change our hypotheses.

From about 1.6 million years BP to 0.5 million years BP, we have a new species that could lay claim to humanity – *Homo erectus*, which is definitely the same genus as modern humans but not the same species: *Homo*, but not *Homo sapiens*. *Homo erectus* evolved in Africa but spread to Eurasia, passing through what is now the Middle East and reaching East Asia and Europe about 1 million years ago. They were about the same size as modern humans with less difference in size between the sexes than was the case with *Australopithecus* (one hypothesis is that the similarity in physical power could correlate with a symmetry in sexual relationships and possibly be an indication of a tendency to monogamy). They hunted medium-to-large game and probably used fire to make meat more digestible, as well as structuring their society into hunting and gathering to improve efficiency. These changes gave them a competitive advantage by increasing the size of group that a piece of land could support. They also made more sophisticated stone tools – Acheulean technology, named after the suburb of Amiens, in France, in which they were first found – which are teardrop-shaped objects chipped from single stones to make cutting edges and points. They are, I think, rather beautiful and I wonder if this is the beginning of art, of someone taking a chip out of the rock not just because it made it a better tool, but because it made it more pleasing to look at and handle.

From about 500,000 to 300,000 years BP we have *Homo heidelbergensis* – a successor (probably descendant) species from *Homo erectus* and ancestor of both Neanderthals and modern humans. They expanded northwards (and get their name from remains found in Germany) using fires, permanent shelters and clothes to enable them to beat the cold. They developed hafting technology – they attached stone spearheads to wooden shafts. We know this because of a find in a lignite mine in Germany where the wood had been preserved by waterlogged conditions that prevented normal decay. They may also have developed language – the traces of which are even harder to dig up than wooden spears. The evidence for this is necessarily circumstantial. First, *Homo heidelbergensis* had a hyoid bone that would have given them a tongue with the dexterity to produce a range of consonants. Second, their middle ear was of a similar sophistication to ours, meaning they heard over a similar frequency range. Third, they seem to have been mostly right-handed, and handedness tends to indicate specialisation in brain function that may be linked to language. As I say, it's all very circumstantial – and raises all kinds of questions about how we know what we say we know about the past (and the answer is that it's nuanced – there's a lot of evidence for some theories, not so much for others: we don't know as much as we would like to, but we know more than nothing – and, as always, there are people out there who know more than I do).

Three hundred thousand years BP marks the end of the Lower Palaeolithic and the first records of *Homo sapiens* – biologically modern humans. The three million years we've spent in the Lower Palaeolithic are to me an indication of how completely mixed up my understanding of history was. The Iron and Bronze Ages each cover around 2000 years of human history (which is a pretty significant span of time for a topic that typically gets less curriculum time than the six years of the Second World War), but there are three main subdivisions of the Stone Age (New, Middle and Old, or Neolithic, Mesolithic and Palaeolithic) and the Palaeolithic is divided into Lower (oldest), Middle and Upper, the first of which covers considerably more hominin history than *Homo sapiens* itself does. Over the preceding three million years we have acquired more and more characteristics that we would now recognise as human: from tool use to innovation, through artistry to language into recognisable communities. Throughout this, the hominin body has evolved until finally we have *Homo sapiens*: the anatomically modern human. Bear with me: we still have a long journey ahead of us before we leave the Old Stone Age. We need to find out how one isolated community of hominins in a corner of Africa came to spread across the world and out-compete every species more closely related than the chimp.

Originally, *Homo sapiens* separated from other *Homo* species in Africa – the ancestors of all modern humans come from this group which then spread out of Africa in waves between about 200,000 and 50,000 years ago. It is difficult to build a clear and definitive narrative here – the most likely theory at the moment seems to be that several early waves got into Eurasia and left remains but were outcompeted by other species and fizzled out. This is another area where one new archaeological find can shift our understanding significantly. While *Homo sapiens* was in Africa, Neanderthals and Denisovans (another group of hominins) lived in Europe and Central Asia respectively. Technological innovations of the time include 'prepared-core tools' in which stone tools were roughly shaped in advance and then tailored to specific tasks when needed. With a prepared core, Stone Age man had a knife, axe, awl and hammer all rolled into one.

We don't know how many groups of early humans left Africa for West Asia but died out before being established, but we do know that the wave of *Homo sapiens* that successfully colonised the planet left Africa around 80,000 years ago and spread swiftly south and east, reaching Australia between 60,000 and 50,000 years ago (tens of thousands of years before the first people reached New Zealand – a geographical distinction that surprised me), Europe slightly later and North America not until the sea levels were favourable – about 20,000 years BP. The evidence for this comes partly from archaeological finds and partly from DNA analysis of modern humans, with mitochondrial DNA (which is passed down the maternal line without mixing) a particularly useful form of information. Groups with similar mitochondrial DNA are called 'haplogroups' and the degree of genetic separation can be used as a sort of clock to give times when populations separated, first within Africa and then across the world. When this wave of *Homo sapiens* met Neanderthal or Denisovan populations they seem to have lived alongside each other and to have reproduced (which has raised a theory that these are three branches of the same species rather than distinct species) – modern humans have both Neanderthal and Denisovan genes. How happily they lived together is unclear – what we know of human history might lead us to believe that the dominant population (who, by definition, became our ancestors) abused the weaker groups. (It has even been suggested that they hunted them for food, albeit with extremely weak justification.) We do, however, know that humans of this period had a varied diet including hunting game, fishing and collecting shellfish (the remains of discarded shells have survived the intervening years).

The final part of our story is the Upper Palaeolithic (Mesolithic and Neolithic history will have to wait for another day). This covers the period 50,000 to 12,000 years BP and the Last Glacial Maximum, in which temperatures across the Northern Hemisphere dropped, reached a minimum and then increased (relatively quickly by Palaeolithic standards, but nowhere near the scale seen in modern times). Improvements in the use of stone tools saw the chips taken from pebbles turned into fine blades, and other tools were developed such as the fish hook, the oil lamp, rope and needles with eyes. This sophistication was possible because groups of humans settled together and individuals were able to become specialists in one task, co-operating rather than being limited by one person doing it all. Meanwhile we have discovered many examples of art, including cave painting and sculpture – among my favourites are the swimming reindeer sculpture that can be found in the British Museum (another of the 100 objects) and the Venus of Hohle Fels. This last is a piece of carved mammoth ivory dated to about 40,000 years BP and is the first known depiction of a human being – although that probably wouldn't be your first guess if you were to glance at it briefly. On more careful examination, what initially looks like a chicken trussed for roasting is an extremely female human statue whose head is several times smaller than her breasts – at which point we should probably reflect how little has changed over the intervening years and draw a line under our investigations.

Rationale and reflections

The overriding purpose of each session is to provoke curiosity, to encourage questions, and so when one group requested a session on the Stone Age I was delighted and felt a responsibility to supply it. It did, however, offer something of a challenge: not only is it an area that I had little prior knowledge about, but it's a huge span of time (even restricting ourselves to the Old Stone Age) and a field of study where evidence is thin and frequently updated, and where conclusions are hotly debated and potentially controversial. (Evolution of humanity, climate change and genetic distinctions of racial groups are the three areas where I've realised I'm talking as an interested amateur but could easily be quoted back at home.)

On the one hand, these are drawbacks that might cause one to back away from the topic, but on the other (and this is the dominant hand), these are all reasons for the idiom of curiosity to push us into wanting to find out more. I've learned a huge amount of pre-history by looking into this, which is both a delight in itself and a good example to students. The limitations of my knowledge (which has come almost entirely from Wikipedia pages, cross-referenced with each other and, occasionally, more scholarly sources) are something I make clear at the beginning of my presentation: 'This is something I'm not an expert in – I've got curious and have read a lot on the internet which I've tried to structure, condense and make sense of for you. I think everything I say is correct, at least as far as anyone knows at this point (and that keeps changing), but if you get told something by someone who is more of an expert than me, please don't say, "Well, Mr Handscombe taught me …". Just come and let me know I was wrong and I'll correct things for the next group.' This is a sort of challenge to some students to go out and get better informed than me (a challenge that would be considerably more difficult in, say, mathematics) with the prize of being able to correct me. So far, I've not been caught out (but I recognise that putting this in print is an invitation to a considerably larger and more informed crowd than I've been playing to thus far – I look forward to becoming better informed).

When putting this presentation together I expected that the most interesting questions would be about hunting woolly mammoths and whether chips in a stone meant a technologically developed tool or just chips in a stone. How wrong! As I delivered the sessions, the curiositometer (some kind of cross between an election swingometer and an infrared detector – still in its development stage but expected to be commercially available by 2035) swung deeply into the red on the evidence for evolution, the difficulty of defining 'human' and the meaning of art. I'll take that. The objective was curiosity, questions rather than answers, and I'd rather students went home with challenging ideas than lived an unexamined life.

The (potential) controversies don't really deserve to be lumped together, so I'll separate them out. Evolution of mankind, to begin with, is a scientific fact, one that is taught in biology and which religions who see things differently have to come to terms with outside the lesson. It is generally a positive thing for it to appear somewhat unexpectedly rather than isolated as a single sequence of lessons taught and forgotten. Some of the richest sources of curiosity (and academic research) come from the liminal edges of subjects where they bleed into each other – of course, knowledge refuses to accept the straitjacket of school disciplines and being able to share this is a strength of the course. The issue has been brought up just once by a student (although I suspect there are others who have felt it as a challenge but not found the words to frame it) who thought it was an interesting session because it was based on certain assumptions – particularly that humans had evolved. I accepted that point – I'd not put forward the evidence for the theory (and don't plan to – there's already a lot to fit into the 40 minutes) and was able to get a better understanding of her thought in one of the freeform discussions (of which more later).

The climate change issue is one that is simply something I'm aware of – I don't want students to get the impression that the changes to the climate that led to the Last Glacial Maximum are of a similar magnitude to those of the twentieth century but, because we're covering 50,000 years as our smallest unit of time, it would be easy to think of things that way. I emphasise the length of time – with the key point being that the Palaeolithic ends about 12,000 years BP, three-quarters of the way through our final 50,000-year chunk. This means that we have, relatively speaking, the blink of an eye to fit in the Mesolithic and Neolithic eras as well as everything that we have been taught as history. Twentieth-century global warming is lightning fast in comparison.

The issue of genetic differences between groups of humans is one I'm careful of because these are ideas that have been used to fuel racism by those who want to do that. It's not something that students have raised, which probably means I'm doing a reasonable job, although I'm aware that they might feel uncomfortable but not feel able to raise it. The science is that there has been so much mixing of humanity over time that the idea of genetically distinct 'races' is unsustainable. (1000 years is approximately enough time to have elapsed that anyone with living descendants would be an ancestor of everybody alive – we all have Genghis Khan in our family trees.) The science also points to haplogroups (which can be of Y-chromosomes passed down the male line as well as maternal mitochondria) that can be used to trace lineages and put dates (in thousands of years) on when they were separated. I plan to refer any students who want to know more to Adam Rutherford's books (see Bibliography).

The final challenge is in making a narrative that is interesting and sufficiently accurate to be informative without disappearing into the detail of academic disputes. When you know only a little about a subject you inevitably fail to realise just how much of that subject there is. I have learned one golden rule, which is to expect there to be a lot. With the Stone Age, I found there was a LOT and have had to work hard to offer students a guide rope to follow and a reason to be interested.

The guide rope I came up with was a timeline to mark off chunks of the 3.3 million years so that we have a constant sense of moving forward, and the reasons to be interested were questions we would seek to answer. Each session of the Cabinet of Curiosity begins with three questions which are designed to be handholds for students to cling to if their grip on the content seems to be failing. They perform a variety of other functions, including sparking intrigue: one such from this session is, 'Who was the Venus of Hohle Fels?' Most initial guesses involve, understandably, a reference to Ancient Greece (which is, of course, far too modern to be relevant). Other questions enable me to assess the starting point of the class and recognise whether I'm facing any experts, in this case a picture of a stone axe and the question, 'What is this for?' So far, I've not found anyone whose personal enthusiasms have crossed significantly with a subject I've been explaining but it's definitely something I worry about and this baseline assessment gives me confidence. A third kind of prompt allows us to reflect on big questions (in this case, 'When did humanity start?') that have no objectively correct answer, but which should provoke opinion, discussion and doubt. Does humanity start with the stone tools? Is it a question of the *Homo* genus? Is it art that is the key human characteristic – or Neil MacGregor's technological drive for improvement? Would it be the first species to look like us? Or to be able to breed with us? Or is it *Homo sapiens*? There are lots of different positions to take and opportunities to get students to make and articulate opinions. (In the case of the Venus of Hohle Fels, do we apply the modern-day attitude of some and assume that a statue of a woman with a tiny head and enormous breasts was made by a man? Or do we consider the competing view that it was made by a woman as part of a fertility cult?)

Chapter 4
British politics 1979–1997 (Or the freedom of idiosyncrasy)

On 3 May 1979, the last election of the 1970s took place after James Callaghan's Labour Government lost a motion of no-confidence. It was politically a significant moment, with the Conservatives using Saatchi and Saatchi to craft their message, 'Labour isn't working', Callaghan carefully insinuating that Margaret Thatcher's sex stopped her being a serious candidate and the BBC using both a swingometer and David Dimbleby to liven proceedings. The issues of the election were inflation, employment, immigration and income tax as well as the impact of the Winter of Discontent, in which the cold weather was exacerbated by a series of strikes.

I remember none of this, although I do remember going with my mother to vote and understanding that this was an important thing to do. I also understood that this was a competition between Margaret and James – which was a particularly useful simplification given that I'm James and my mother is Margaret. I was, of course, supporting Callaghan – we Jameses have to stick together.

Unfortunately for both me and the Labour Party, this was Thatcher's first victory – she came to power with an entirely workable majority of 43 (a significant change from the wafer-thin majorities and hung parliaments of the decade's previous elections). The election map of the UK, however, looked considerably bluer than this due to a concentration of Conservative seats in rural (and therefore less densely populated) areas and the Labour dominance in small, city constituencies. The Liberals had 11 seats scattered across the country, the SNP were reduced to two seats, Plaid Cymru got one and Northern Ireland, as always, had its own parties.

The first few years of the Thatcher Government were difficult economically and made the Conservatives extremely unpopular. There was an international recession and, locally, the Government brought in reforms that had the impact of making imports cheaper and local industry less economically viable, which caused a huge number of job losses in such areas as mining and manufacturing. Inflation, which had peaked at 22% in 1980, came down but unemployment reached 12.5% in 1982 and far higher than this in industrialised parts of the country such as Northern Ireland and Tyneside. The idea that there would be a second election victory seemed ridiculous, despite Michael Foot's leadership moving Labour far to the left of where much of the country felt comfortable.

In January 1981, the Labour conference committed to unilateral nuclear disarmament and withdrawal from the European Economic Community. Moderates in the party responded to this by breaking away to form a new party, the Social Democratic Party (SDP), which formed an electoral alliance with the Liberals. Together, they were a strong centrist bloc that operated throughout the 1980s until the two parties merged to form the Liberal Democrats. By the end of 1981, the SDP had picked up 28 MPs defecting from the Labour Party (and one from the Conservatives) and the Alliance was polling at 50%. There was a strange mood in political discourse – a sense of the end of an era and the start of something new.

Then, on 2 April 1982, Argentinian forces invaded and occupied the Falkland Islands and South Georgia, at least partly to bolster the limited legitimacy of General Galtieri's military junta, but also in response to a lack of diplomatic progress over Argentina's long-running claim to the islands (the process having been held up by the robust preference of Falkland Islanders for British rule). There followed 74 days of war in which a British naval task force retook the islands.

I was old enough to follow this story on *Newsround*, although not old enough to understand either the incredible logistics of conducting a war on the far side of the world or the horror that goes with war. I followed the story through the numbers of casualties, sunk ships and Exocet missiles fired, feeling patriotically buoyed when the data seemed to favour the British. On 14 June, the Argentine forces on the islands surrendered and Thatcher's boldness in contesting the invasion had been justified at the cost of 900 lives, 16 ships and 135 aircraft between the two sides.

The issues of a splintering Labour Party and a war victory meant that Thatcher was confident enough to call an election in 1983, a year before she needed to. They also led to a decisive victory and a majority of 144 seats. Despite receiving 25% of the popular vote, the Alliance gained only 23 seats. Labour, with 2% more, had 209 seats because its support was concentrated in its industrial heartland towns of the north of England, South Wales and the central belt of Scotland. First-past-the-post has a lot to answer for.

If the Falklands War was a news story that was simple enough for me to follow, then the miners' strike of 1984–85 was one that I could hardly avoid. It was one of the most bitter industrial disputes in British history and, over the span of a year, resulted in 26 million lost person-days of work, the largest figure since the General Strike of 1926. My memories are of nightly news footage of violent confrontations between the police and strikers, with a huge amount of anger at the damage that had been done to mining communities by government policy and the inexorable march of technological progress.

Coal mining in the UK peaked in 1922 and had been declining since then due to machinery replacing workers, cheaper imports and a reduced reliance on coal as it was replaced by oil and gas for some purposes. The reduction flattened out during the Second World War and, despite heavy national subsidies, dropped sharply in the 1960s before strikes in 1972 and 1974 brought down Edward Heath's Conservative Government and forced a rethink. Thatcher reversed this policy of propping up the British coal industry and made plans to resist a rerun of the earlier strikes: she stockpiled coal and made plans to use police to enable those who wanted to work to do so, while ensuring that the economic impact of striking would fall heavily on the strikers (the 1980 Social Security Act reduced the support available to the dependents of striking workers).

Meanwhile, the National Union of Mineworkers (NUM) ran a closed shop – which prevented the pits from employing non-union workers – and, led by Arthur Scargill, who championed left-wing and militant union policies, overestimated the strength of its position. From Thatcher's point of view, the economics of the case were straightforward: British coal was 25% more expensive than importing it from abroad, and this was despite subsidies from the government that meant the taxpayer was paying to have it dug out of the ground. Her government decided that this had to be resolved, and uneconomic pits closed, if the economy was to recover.

In March 1984, she announced that 20 collieries would close with the loss of 20,000 jobs.

Scargill misjudged the situation and declared a strike. In doing so he underestimated Thatcher's preparations and determination, which included provoking a strike in March when reliance on coal for heating was reducing. The NUM also lost public support (including from some miners) by failing to take a national ballot. As the strike went on, union payments to striking miners dried up and hunger forced even some of the most vehement back to work. The strike continued until March 1985 when the NUM split, a new Union of Democratic Mineworkers was set up and miners in the targeted pits accepted redundancy payments.

As a coda to this part of the story, my first teaching job (in 1999) was in what had been the mining town of Tonypandy in South Wales – where pit closures had preceded the strike – and the loss was still felt. Mining had given pride to the workers in a way that call-centre or even production-line factory work did not. Unemployment was high and hope was low (which made teaching even more of a challenge than it usually is). Meanwhile, my wife was working in a hospital in Swansea and was struck by the high levels of lung disease not seen elsewhere – the effects of coal-dust inhalation could be seen as clearly in her work as the impact of pit closures could in mine.

The Conservatives' popularity had dropped during the miners' strike but despite this, and Labour having replaced Michael Foot with the (comparatively) young and (relatively) attractive Neil Kinnock, Thatcher confidently called for an election in 1987 (again after only four, rather than five, years). The Conservatives ran a campaign on the economy, which was beginning to be cheerful news with inflation down to 4% and unemployment finally dropping below three million, and defence, where they argued that a party that believed in unilateral disarmament could not be trusted with keeping the country safe. They also argued that Labour couldn't be trusted on social issues, using attack posters on the teaching of homosexuality and claiming that children as young as five would be shown 'how it was done' with the aid of brightly coloured stick men.

The election went badly for the opposition, with the Conservative majority only slightly reduced to 102 as Labour picked up 20 seats, the Alliance lost one and the SNP and Plaid Cymru both gained one. Thatcher became the first party leader to win three consecutive elections in 150 years and the country became even more divided, with the Conservative hold on Southern England (including most of London) strengthening as they lost seats elsewhere. The 1987 election is also notable for the election of Diane Abbott, Paul Boateng and Bernie Grant, the first black MPs to come to Westminster since the 1800s.

Despite the large majority, Thatcher's third term was not easy: there was tension in the Conservative Party over Europe (the key debate was over whether or not to join the Exchange Rate Mechanism); the economy was cooling, with interest rates pushed up to 15% as inflation rose to 10%; and the Community Charge (poll tax) was deeply unpopular. In 1989, she faced a leadership challenge (the first since she became party leader in 1975) from Sir Anthony Meyer, whose status as an entirely unserious candidate was underlined when he gained 33 out of 374 votes and slipped back into insignificance. What was not insignificant was that Thatcher only gained 314 of the votes, with 27 spoiling their ballots or not voting at all. Michael Heseltine, a former Cabinet minister whose role for the past few years had been to sit on the back benches growling forebodingly, growled forebodingly that something would have to change.

A year passed in which very little did change, at least to Heseltine's way of thinking, and so on 14 November 1990 he issued a leadership challenge to Thatcher. The rules of the time meant there could be up to three rounds of voting, each with a different procedure.

1 To win in the first round, a candidate needed an absolute majority of votes and to exceed the closest opponent by at least 15% of the MPs.
2 New candidates could be proposed to join a second round of voting which would finish things if one candidate gained 50% of the vote; otherwise all but the top three would be knocked out.
3 The third round would be run under an Alternative Vote system – if no candidate gained 50% of first-choice votes, the ballot papers that had the third candidate as favourite would be reallocated to the candidate marked as second favourite.

In the first round of voting on 20 November, Thatcher, possibly confident of victory, was in Paris. She won convincingly, by 204 votes to 152, but was four votes short of the required 15%. She declared her intention of fighting on, but on the morning of 22 November my A-level chemistry teacher arrived slightly late to class to let us know that Margaret Thatcher had resigned as prime minister. We said to ourselves that this was our Kennedy moment (referring to his assassination almost exactly 27 years earlier) and that we would always remember where we were when we heard Thatcher had resigned. On that count it seems that I was right (although I can't remember what chemistry we studied that day – perhaps the lesson was taken over by political ramification and rumination).

After Thatcher's resignation, two Cabinet ministers, Douglas Hurd and John Major, declared their candidacy and in the second round, Major made a convincing showing with 185 votes to Heseltine's 131. Hurd had just enough votes (56) to prevent a victory at this point but both he and Heseltine dropped out, rendering the third round unnecessary, and John Major became prime minister in what seemed to my chemistry class to be a caretaker role, seeing out the last few months of the Conservative Government.

Major had to call an election before June 1992 and, in a decision that infuriated the 17-year-old me, went for 9 April, just two weeks before I would have been old enough to vote. It was a campaign that, nevertheless, I was very interested in – the Alliance had been replaced by the Liberal Democrats and there was every chance of a hung parliament. Kinnock was still leading Labour and had cleared up a lot of their left-wing image, and, at the very least, this was the first election for years that Margaret Thatcher had no chance of winning.

The smart money may have been on a small Labour majority or a Labour government in a pact with the Lib Dems, but that's not how it ended up. Commentators are unable to decide whether it was the result of a headline in *The Sun* ('If Kinnock wins today will the last person to leave Britain please turn out the lights'), a strange rally Kinnock held in Sheffield (in which he repeatedly called out the phrase 'We're [or well] alright') or possibly the successes of Major's early years, including the first Gulf War and the Maastricht Treaty. For whatever reason, more people voted for the Conservatives in 1992 than have ever voted for any party in a general election before or since (a figure that actually represents the intersection of increasing population and decreasing turnout rather than any particular popularity) and they gained a small but workable majority of 21. Commentators may be divided on the reasons for this, but *The Sun* immediately claimed responsibility with the headline, 'It's the Sun wot won it'.

The Conservatives lost 40 seats and Labour gained the same number, the Liberal Democrats held onto the same number of seats the Alliance had in 1987 and Plaid Cymru picked up a fourth seat in Wales.

Over the next five years, the Government's slender majority was eroded as they lost all eight by-elections caused by the death of Conservative

MPs, faced rebellion over Europe in which ten MPs lost the whip for a period of time, and saw MPs defect to the opposition (two to the Liberal Democrats, one to Labour and one, for the space of two weeks before the general election, to the Referendum Party). Meanwhile, a succession of scandals involving Conservative MPs and ministers further eroded trust in Major's Government – this was particularly damaging under Major's 'Back to Basics' programme to push for socially conservative values which gave the media (and, if I'm honest, teenagers) an excuse to gossip about a succession of adulterous affairs and closeted homosexuality (something that Section 28 of the Local Government Act had made it illegal for my teachers to educate me about). In addition to these, Michael Mates resigned after supporting Asil Nadir, a fugitive businessman later convicted on ten counts of theft; Alan Duncan exploited the 'Right to Buy' scheme for council-house residents in order to acquire a second home from his elderly next-door neighbour; Tim Smith and Neil Hamilton resigned in the 'cash for questions' scandal in which they were accused of taking money and gifts from Mohamed al-Fayed for asking parliamentary questions (something Smith admitted and Hamilton denied, going on to lose a libel case over the affair and being investigated by the Conservative Party); and Jonathan Aitken resigned as Chief Secretary to the Treasury in order to sue *The Guardian* and ITV, in the process of which he lied under oath and was imprisoned for perjury.

By the time 1997 came along, Tony Blair was Labour leader, John Major's Government no longer had a majority and we were all bored by scandal. I was at university in America and so cast my vote by proxy – in a nice closure of the circle, my mother cast it for me. The election was a resounding Labour victory with a majority of 179 and a Conservative Party reduced to Southern England (with no Scottish or Welsh seats and only 12 MPs north of the Humber). The Liberal Democrats (under Paddy Ashdown) leaped to 46 seats, the SNP doubled their total to six and the number of female MPs increased from 60 to 120, but the story that most grabbed my attention (apart from the fact that my vote clearly made a strategic difference in the constituency of Sheffield Hallam as the sitting MP was defeated) was in Tatton, Cheshire. This was a safe Conservative seat held by Neil Hamilton, whose denial of corruption was wearing thin but who refused to step down and appeared to have a bombproof majority. This thesis was tested to destruction when Martin Bell, a BBC war reporter, stood as an independent candidate against him. Labour and the Liberal Democrats both withdrew their candidates and Bell won a resounding victory, with a majority of 11,000 (in what had been the fourth safest Conservative seat) – the first successful independent candidate since 1951. Martin Bell, himself not bombproof as he had been injured reporting from a war zone a few years earlier, wins a 'bombproof' constituency. How newspaper sub-editors must love that kind of thing.

Rationale and reflections

An inexhaustive internet search has led me to the conclusion that the boundary between history and current affairs is not well defined. A pragmatic approach is to say that history is whatever is taught in schools and universities under the heading of 'History'. Pragmatic but unsatisfying, still there is some justification here. Set courses require examinations and an examiner will want the student to have sufficient well-researched texts to draw on when they compose their essays. This definition leads us to agree that pre-history (covered in chapter 3) is that period that comes before such a wealth of considered texts. History, of course, is what happened in the past and current affairs is what is happening now, in my lifetime. But lifetime is subjective. For my nephew, the Second World War is ancient history; for my father-in-law, it is what was going on when he was a toddler. The 'lifetime' approach gives what I might term high and low watermarks, with the sea being the past and the beach the present. For the generation below me, history lies beyond the high watermark; for the one before me, it's further away. My students and I lie somewhere in between and the gap between us is an interestingly liminal space: too recent to be fully developed into school history but long enough ago that only one person in the room can remember it.

History sufficiently recent that it falls into 'current affairs' for the teacher is something that's rarely covered in school but the period immediately preceding the students' birth is an interesting one: a time of which they have no personal knowledge but from which they can get an eye-witness account (with all the strengths and limitations of that format). The exploration of this tidal space is a good opportunity for curiosity because these events have shaped the present and because the period provides a provocation to be interested in what's happening now. For any students of domestic politics, this provocation would have been especially apparent as it has taken little imagination to draw a parallel between the tail end of Major's Government and the Conservatives in the early 2020s. For those more interested in international affairs, episodes of *The West Wing* from 25 years ago are similarly prescient, with both the issues of populism and the situation in Gaza looking unchanged.

The idiosyncratic approach I take is to tell this story through my own memories of the time. Technically, the gap between my birth and that of the students is from the early seventies to the early noughties but I have narrowed it down to 1979–97. This is not just a pleasing symmetry – it's also the time from the first election I remember to the first one I voted in. The structure I use is to look at the elections that took place in this period and in particular to look at the election maps, recognising the colours of the parties, the typical distribution of seats and the misleading impact of geography whereby less densely occupied areas of the country have larger constituencies (by area) and therefore appear to be more important.

Despite the high level of content, this session tends to go well: students are interested in how elections work and have heard stories of Margaret Thatcher's time in government but generally as disconnected anecdotes or diatribes rather than a continuous narrative. Framing the story through my own experience highlights the aspects that were accessible and interesting to me at the time, and therefore creates natural parallels with their experience of politics, the stories that have seemed accessible and interesting during their lifetimes.

Providing some context for current politics and conveying a slice of late twentieth-century history are reasons enough to deliver a session like this, but the real benefit, I think, is that the story enables some relationship-building with the class (which is difficult in one session a week for eight weeks) without (I hope) being too self-indulgent, because the Conservative governments of Thatcher and Major are worthy of curiosity in themselves. There are two kinds of curiosity stimulated here – some are interested in the human story of the small boy who grew up to be their teacher (especially in the more ridiculous aspects of that small boy), and some want to know what happened before Blair's downfall and the Brown years which are their earliest personal political memories.

The two stories I pick up on are particularly valuable for raising big questions and leaving the students with thoughts to pick up on later. The miners' strike illustrates the difficulty of political decision making while the leadership challenge brings to life something about how government actually works.

The key challenge that I try to convey in the miners' strike is that two things can be true: the pits were vital to the lives of the communities built round them but they were also a really expensive way for the government to kill its people. A union slogan was 'When they close a pit, they kill a community' and the ruthless policing, the single-minded focus on macroeconomic indicators at the expense of individuals, their work and careers, and the cold strategy with which the Government planned for the strike, all give weight to the feeling that Thatcher's Government was unsympathetic to this plight. On the other hand, when the industry required hefty taxpayer subsidies and still produced coal that was more expensive than that produced elsewhere and shipped to the UK, and when the industry was both immediately dangerous in terms of mining accidents and a long-term health risk in terms of lung damage, it's difficult to defend any other decision on the basis of a cost–benefit analysis. Politics is often portrayed as a left versus right, or right versus wrong, situation whereas the blacks and whites of that portrayal fade into a much more difficult grey when you get into the detail.

The end of Thatcher's time as prime minister is interesting because it seemed to be very sudden, an announcement in a chemistry lesson, but actually there were reasons, structures and rules that were followed, as well as personalities and egos that played a huge part. The poll tax and Europe loomed off stage, but Thatcher had been unpopular before. The difference this time was the coincidence of Meyer's willingness to expose a chink in her armour, Heseltine waiting in the wings, keen to seize any opportunity, and maybe (this can be endlessly debated) some exhaustion on her part. Having dragged the country out of the 1970s, having won three elections, it would be strange if there wasn't part of her thinking 'not again', reacting against the ingratitude of a party that she had led to such success. The myth unpicked here is that politics is an intellectual pursuit of ideas and policies and it can be surprising to recognise how much comes down to coincidence and human frailty. (As I write this, the news stories are filled with the incidents and accidents of the first months of Trump's second presidency – perhaps it will be a long time before we have the luxury of falling for this particular myth.)

The two stories are good ones, but they are not the only ones that could be used to make those points – I have chosen them because they struck me at the time, because they have resonated with me personally. The central idea of the Cabinet of Curiosity is that we are all interested in different things for a wealth of different reasons and when I share my curiosities with the class I'm not, primarily, saying that I think this is what they should be interested in (although I am trying to demonstrate that sharing someone else's curiosity can be a pleasing and informative pastime and am delighted when one of them wants to take things further). Instead, I'm hinting at a world filled with things that are worth knowing more about and suggesting that you need very little excuse to start learning.

The news stories of my childhood and the way they resonated with me are so obviously personal ways into this story that I'm not inviting the students to follow in my footsteps but rather encouraging them to follow the glimpses that have opened up in their own lives.

I am also trying to make news, and hard news rather than sport and celebrity, seem both accessible and worth following up. The modern world is not one in which the reading of physical newspapers is likely to see a resurgence, but there are more and less serious vehicles for current affairs. I don't explicitly tell them to listen to the BBC, to read the *Financial Times* and *New York Times*, to search out serious journalists and commentators (perhaps I should, although I think it's difficult to do that without reflecting my own biases and without making the whole process sound boring and worthy) – rather, I'm trying to awaken a hunger for something beyond headlines and clickbait, hoping that if that's awoken then they will go looking for content that will feed it. (I am, of course, happy to provide recommendations to any student who asks.) 'What's going on, and why?' are questions that can be asked of every news story, every situation in the world – current affairs provide an endless opportunity for curiosity.

Chapter 5
Art appreciation for beginners (Or why interactivity beats lectures every time)

I'm not an artist – painting always seemed like the least fun thing one could do with numbers and anything more sophisticated than that has been beyond me. Art history is therefore a glorious field in which to exercise my curiosity – what do artists do, what is it that is clever about painting, what about it is interesting? What makes one artist better than, or even different from, another? Explore with me the work of two of my favourite painters.

John Constable and J.M.W. Turner (who was known by the name William) were English landscape painters of the Romantic school and first half of the nineteenth century. Constable was born in Suffolk and was expected to take over the family corn-trading business; Turner was born in London and his father was a barber who, from early on, boasted that his son would be a painter.

Constable's landscape painting career began with depictions of country estates for their wealthy owners – *Wivenhoe Park* (1816) is an example of this genre and shows some typical Constable features: still water, broad skies and a rural idyll, in this case a fine house just outside Colchester.

Arguably the defining works of his career, however, are the six-foot canvases painted in the early 1820s that include his most famous painting, *The Hay Wain*. This shows a horse-drawn wagon standing in a stream in the English countryside. The river is the Stour, which forms the border between Suffolk (on the left) and Essex, and one explanation for the rather strange parking spot is that wagon drivers would want to give their horses a drink and also to cool their wheels in the midday sun. (An early title given by Constable was 'Landscape: noon'.) It was originally unappreciated in England but praised in France (where it charmed Théodore Géricault and inspired Eugène Delacroix). It is now one of Britain's favourite paintings and hangs in the National Gallery alongside another of Constable's paintings, *The Cornfield* – also originally exhibited, in 1826, under the title 'Landscape: noon', which must tell us something about Constable's linguistic imagination.

Both paintings display an eye for detail and an impressive realism. One critic said that Constable showed his viewers the truth – the trees are so intricate that you fancy each individual leaf can be picked out and white fluffy clouds decorate the sky. The landscapes are, however, artificial – Constable wasn't painting a wilderness, but the heavily farmed fields of his home county; nor was he above taking liberties with the scenery for the sake of a good composition.

My favourite Constable painting (apart from *The Hay Wain*, a print of which hung in my grandparents' living room and is now in my study) is *Salisbury Cathedral from the Meadows*, painted in 1831, on display in Tate Britain, and described by some critics as the climax of his artistic career: Constable himself said that it best embodied the full compass of his art. In it the familiar trees, clouds, English countryside and horses standing in a peaceful stream are joined by the eponymous cathedral and a rather remarkable rainbow. There's a lot to look at, a lot of detail to marvel at, and even a philistine such as myself can see that there's a real skill in painting a rainbow as it is rather than as the picture books of your childhood taught you to think of it.

One early work of J.M.W. Turner is entitled *Calais Pier* and depicts a group of ships (some under sail, some rowed) on a rough sea with a busy wooden pier in the foreground. It illustrates some of the differences between Turner and Constable while sharing some common roots. As in the Constable paintings, the sky is a significant feature, with carefully worked clouds, and again we see a depiction of water (a feature of landscape painting I find particularly interesting – it's not obvious to me how one should go about painting a clear transparent liquid and I find the decisions made by expert artists in doing so repay careful study). However, the streams and pools painted by Constable were peaceful while Turner's sea is anything but; the clouds are more tempestuous and even the people are more active, battling against the elements rather than pausing tranquilly.

Constable was disappointed in *Calais Pier*, saying that it was 'more extravagant and less attentive to detail', but Turner showed no inclination to remedy this 'fault' in paintings such as *Ulysses Deriding Polyphemus – Homer's Odyssey* from 1829. This is a painting of a ship at sea but beyond that there are few details that leap to the eye: the canvas is a maelstrom of colour with the low sun illuminating both the clouds and the water in a riot of reds, yellows and oranges. The figure of Ulysses can just be made out on the ship but I'm not at all sure about Polyphemus. (I'm willing to take Turner's word that he's there somewhere.)

The story of Ulysses and Polyphemus is told in Homer's *Odyssey*: the titular hero (Odysseus is the Greek name, Ulysses the Latin) has landed on a strange island as he makes his way home from Troy (in what is now Turkey) to his home in Ithaca, off the west coast of Greece. The island is home to the Cyclopes, giants with just one eye, who live an apparently peaceful and pastoral life farming sheep when they are not disturbed by passing heroes. One Cyclops, Polyphemus, captures Odysseus and his crew and plans to eat the sailors as a way of enlivening his diet and reducing wear and tear on his flock. Odysseus puts Polyphemus' eye out with a wooden spike, declares his name is 'Nobody' and escapes with his remaining men on the underside of the sheep as they file past Polyphemus to graze in the morning. Polyphemus wails in distress: 'Nobody has hurt me', 'Nobody is escaping', 'Nobody has made me look ridiculous'. His brother Cyclopes are all reassured by this news and fail to come to his aid, allowing the Greeks to escape to their ship and make fun of the hapless giant. Polyphemus also appears in Virgil's *Aeneid*, a later poem about a later voyage visiting the same island, in which he is memorably described as '*monstrum horrendum, informe, ingens, cui lumen ademptum*' – the horrible monster, deformed and huge, whose eye has been put out.

So, William Turner imagines a scene from an ancient Greek story and … Well, the 'and' is rather interesting. In 1815, Mount Tambora, in present-day Indonesia, erupted with the most powerful eruption in recorded human history. This event fired enough ash into the atmosphere to affect the global climate, leading to an exceptionally poor summer in 1816 and consequent crop failures and hardship (as well as a disappointing summer holiday for the Shelleys and consequent writing of *Frankenstein*). The sun filtering through ash-filled skies inspired painters, including Turner, to depict spectacular sunsets, such as the one in *Ulysses Deriding Polyphemus*. Perhaps the best known one forms the backdrop for *The Fighting Temeraire*. When the nation is polled on its favourite paintings, *The Fighting Temeraire* is the one that nudges *The Hay Wain* into second place. It was painted in 1838 and shows the final journey of one of Nelson's warships – the *Temeraire* – pulled by a steam tug to the docks at Rotherhithe, in south-east London, to be broken up for scrap. The elements of sky and water dominate again and the tug belches orange smoke in the foreground. The *Temeraire* herself is picked out in white, an almost ghostly shape fading into the background, sails furled, and the symbolism of the replacement of the beautiful and valiant past by an ugly and functional future is haunting. The sun sets on the age of sail and we are towed unwillingly into an age of steam.

The Fighting Temeraire is an arresting painting and I can see why it is a popular favourite but it is not Turner's last word on steam power and I think that *Rain, Steam, and Speed – The Great Western Railway* from 1844 is even more remarkable. If Salisbury Cathedral was the culmination of Constable's skill in depicting the countryside with careful and attentive realism then *Rain, Steam, and Speed* is the zenith of Turner's obsession with the intangible. It remains a landscape painting of the English countryside, specifically the Great Western Railway crossing the river Thames on Brunel's bridge at Maidenhead, but all physical detail is sacrificed to giving the impression of light and moving water and the speed of the onrushing train. Entirely extravagant and lacking in detail – it's almost as though Turner took Constable's criticism as a challenge.

Turner and Constable were contemporaries, observing the same changing world but recording it very differently. Constable was determined to put down in oils exactly what he saw of a placid, unchanging pastoral England that he must have recognised was disappearing, while Turner seems to me to have been trying to capture the rapid development on a still canvas. Constable represents the peak of realistic landscape painting while I see Turner as the first modern artist, creating impressionism in *Rain, Steam, and Speed* 28 years before Monet's painting, *Impression, Sunrise*, gave it a name.

Rationale and reflections

I call this session 'Art appreciation for beginners'. Perhaps a more honest title would be 'Art appreciation by a beginner', which is appropriate on many levels, not least that you don't need to know anything to appreciate art – you just need to look. Meanwhile, it's such a broad canvas (sorry) that there's something for everybody – trying to work out which paintings and artists we, personally, enjoy is an excellent way to develop some curiosity.

For the purposes of the session, I selected two contemporaries from the nineteenth century. Two seemed to work as I could make comparisons yet not overcomplicate. Which two is arbitrary; you just need some points of similarity and some points of difference. Manet and Monet would work (both French artists of the nineteenth century) and you have the added bonus here of past TV programmes and the general web interest because of the close similarity of their names. It might be harder if you choose Van Dyck and Van Gogh. I went closer to home: I chose two English painters.

As I happily admitted at the outset, I am not an artist or an art teacher. I have a layman's enthusiasm and this session, as much as any, always shows how useful enthusiasm is in choosing a subject and how valuable it can be in its delivery.

It's easy for fine art to be thought of as 'posh' or too difficult for teenagers to access (this thinking being often done by the teenagers themselves as they look for more easily digestible forms of culture). Barriers, though, do exist, and if our objective is to increase curiosity then some way of getting over, through or round the barriers is needed. I hope that my naïve enthusiasm carries the unspoken message that you don't have to be an art expert to enjoy art. Looking at beautiful things is a privilege, but this privilege can be open to all – many galleries have free entry. Maybe, though, you need a little bit of knowledge and confidence as a companion to enable you to make your way through the door. One of the barriers to art appreciation is not knowing enough to get a handle on what you're looking at, or looking for – maybe you recognise that you like some paintings more than others, but why that is and how you can see more of the 'good' ones is difficult to know without knowing a little about what you see.

By introducing two great landscape painters, identifying their differences and the progression of their work, I think this lesson provides a starting point for looking at art. Sometimes my curious students will get lucky when they go into a gallery and see a painting they recognise (they now have eight more than they did), sometimes they will be able to spot a Constable or a Turner, but even if not they can start thinking, 'Is it earlier or later than the paintings I know?' And even if they don't get that right, they have got some language for articulating their understanding.

The lesson tends to be fun because all students have to make a guess about whether the paintings are by the same artist or a different one – there's no hiding behind others. And it's a good set of questions to make guesses on; somehow this feels low stakes as there can be no shame in being wrong, partly because you have about half the class with you and partly because who on earth is meant to know about random painters from two centuries ago? It also allows me to be enthusiastic about what I'm showing them – I recognise that my tastes are not terribly obscure (given that the nation's two favourite paintings are on my list) but they are expressed through gesticulation, superlatives and big smiles.

This session also allows some digressions into history – it's particularly useful to think about the Industrial Revolution happening during this time and the different reactions of Constable and Turner: Constable retires into the nostalgia of a rural idyll while Turner, possibly also wistfully, tries to recreate the scene of the present hurtling towards the future. There is also geography (via Mount Tambora), literature (*Frankenstein*) and Classics (Latin or Greek or both).

Final comment. This diversity of 'hooks' brings me back to my earlier point that one of the great values of curiosity is that answering one question often leads you to ask several more. The intertextuality and self-referential nature of art is such that satisfying our interest in early nineteenth-century art could open a cabinet filled with a whole range of curious stories.

Chapter 6
The Second Coming by W.B. Yeats
(Or why you can start with what you know but can't stay there)

My knowledge of poetry is not extensive compared with my English-teaching colleagues and my taste for it has developed almost entirely in the decade that Harris Westminster has been operational – it has been my go-to field when I've felt the need to demonstrate my fascination with learning because committing a poem to memory is not only a neat trick in itself, but also brings you a considerable step closer to really understanding what the poet is getting at. As a poem consists entirely of words, focusing on those words is, if not the only way to come to grips with it, at least one effective approach.

One of my English-teaching colleagues told me that Yeats' *The Second Coming* is the second greatest poem of the twentieth century and since there's no more objective approach than personal preference, I took him at his word. I am also fond of the one he ranked above this (*Church Going* by Philip Larkin, which made a fleeting appearance in chapter 1), but it is rather longer and so when I reach into the cabinet looking for verse, this is what I pluck out.

The Second Coming

Turning and turning in the widening gyre
The falcon cannot hear the falconer;
Things fall apart; the centre cannot hold;
Mere anarchy is loosed upon the world,
The blood-dimmed tide is loosed, and everywhere
The ceremony of innocence is drowned;
The best lack all conviction, while the worst
Are full of passionate intensity.

Surely some revelation is at hand;
Surely the Second Coming is at hand.
The Second Coming! Hardly are those words out
When a vast image out of Spiritus Mundi
Troubles my sight: somewhere in sands of the desert
A shape with lion body and the head of a man,
A gaze blank and pitiless as the sun,
Is moving its slow thighs, while all about it
Reel shadows of the indignant desert birds.
The darkness drops again; but now I know
That twenty centuries of stony sleep
Were vexed to nightmare by a rocking cradle,
And what rough beast, its hour come round at last,
Slouches towards Bethlehem to be born?

William Butler Yeats was an Irish poet and Nobel Laureate of the late nineteenth and early twentieth century. His early work is illuminated by Irish folk tales and mythology but he became more political, and his work more realistic, in later years. Politically, he was an Irish Nationalist who served as a Senator of the Irish Free State in the 1920s.

This poem was written in 1919 when the world was recovering from the First World War, Yeats' wife was recovering from the Spanish flu that followed it and Ireland was heading into the Irish War of Independence. It's a poem that captures a sense of foreboding and which resurfaced in the popular consciousness in 2016 (I suspect it never went away among poetry-lovers). The ideas have resonated with every class I've taught it to since.

The first stanza imagines a falconer. I see him on the top of a hill surrounded by wide sky and a wild land with quite a wind blowing. The falcon is out hunting, circling above, sweeping out an ever-widening arc until it can no longer hear the call of the falconer – the auditory thread that had held the bird in check breaks and there's nothing to pull it back to the centre. In the usual way of things this might result in a temporarily lost falcon, but we are clearly in the middle of a metaphor for Yeats immediately tells us that 'anarchy' and a 'blood-dimmed tide' are let loose; a wave of death that drowns 'the ceremony of innocence' – perhaps we are to imagine the rituals and routines of everyday life.

The next two lines are the poem's most famous couplet and every time I read them I'm left unsure whether they are a definition or a complaint. Is Yeats saying that those who carry doubt in their hearts are better than the extremists who cannot be swayed from their conviction; or is he bewailing the observed state of affairs that those he thinks worthy are dithering while less competent leaders push their agenda forward against inadequate opposition? Maybe both, but it's here that the rise of extremism across Europe and America makes the poem feel current. Can our centre ground of politics hold? That, of course, is really a different discussion for another day, one where dissenting voices can hold as much sway as mine. On to the second stanza.

We have an immediate injection of pace, and an immediate injection of Christian imagery. In this falling-apart world we're all looking for an answer, or possibly the apocalypse: 'revelation' meaning both, via the last book of the Bible whose common title is Revelation and whose subject matter is the end of the world. We hope for an answer to a falling-apart world, an answer that doesn't imply an apocalypse, but we seek simple answers – we're drawn to the answers of passionate intensity rather than the nuance of, 'I'm not sure'. Is this what Yeats is saying? Well, I'm not sure – I'm not sure he's sure. As I promised at the start, we can look at the words and we're grabbed by the title of the poem, *The Second Coming*, and the statement, assertion, cry that it is surely at hand. As soon as this realisation hits Yeats, he's sucked into a vision – one that he claims comes out of the '*Spiritus Mundi*' – the spirit of the world, or perhaps we might say the spirit of the age.

He sees a desert somewhere with a vast and stony statue with the body of a lion and the head of a man. It seems clear that we're meant to be imagining the Sphinx and therefore a location in Egypt. This statue is, however, moving and even though it's doing so slowly it is menacing: its gaze is 'blank and pitiless' and the movement surprises the birds (quite reasonably if they had been resting on it) and they rise and circle above it. That's it for the vision – 'The darkness drops'. It's just a glimpse of a threat that had been dormant but is now on the move, and it's an image that shifts our focus from the British (or Irish) hillside where we started into the Middle East. Egypt is not the location of events in Revelation – according to that book the final battle will be at a place called Armageddon, perhaps meaning Mount Megiddo in Israel. The shape is, however, on the move and the impression is that it is inexorable.

The poet concludes by offering his deductions from the vision. Now he knows that the 'stony sleep' that had protected the world for the 2000 years since the first coming has ended and that the Sphinx, or whatever threat it represents, is coming to Bethlehem, not hurrying but slouching its way slowly to where the new age will be born. The mention of Bethlehem is clearly a reference to the birth of Jesus, which took place in Bethlehem, after which, according to one of the accounts, he and his family went to Egypt to escape slaughter. Maybe Yeats is imagining the second coming as the first in some kind of reverse.

The imagery is threatening: this is not a baby in a stable, not an era of peace that we are being offered, but a massacre, a 'blood-dimmed tide'. It is also inevitable: there's no sense that this rough beast can be stopped – its hour has finally come round.

Rationale and reflections

Often the student experience of poetry is focused on what needs to be learned from their anthology for GCSE rather than what their teacher loves, and so there tends to be a sizeable proportion of students that have decided that poetry is not for them. Been there, seen it, done it, memorised a few lines. Poetry is boring. This can happen even when they have come across a poem-loving teacher who has managed to inveigle their favourites into the curriculum, or even a teacher who presents as someone who finds the curriculum filled with the most marvellous gems of poetic felicity. In *How to Be Topp* (2009; first published 1954) by Geoffrey Willans, the hero Molesworth tells us about this experience in his own, regrettable, style: 'Sometimes english masters make you read poems chiz chiz chiz. You have to sa the weedy words and speke them beatifully as if you knew what they meant. Fotherington-tomas thinks this is absolutely super and when he sa he wander lonely as a cloud you think he will flote out of the window.'

Part of the point of this session is that poetry is simply too wonderful to be left to English teachers and Fotherington-Thomas, and that I, as a mathematician, am able to explain that I, too, once thought that poetry was not for me, until I actually put some time into learning some poems. This is not to say that I explain poetry better than English teachers but rather that students suspend their prejudice, they cut me some slack. In short, they are curious to find out what the maths guy thinks about weedy words chiz chiz.

It is therefore important that the poem I deliver is one of my favourites; I'm back to building on enthusiasms. Choosing something I think is amazing is far more important than the actual poem itself (although I have selected from my favourites one that has some difficult imagery and relevance to our current lives, and one that is relatively short – short enough for a single session to explore all the words, if not the marvellous depth of ideas). I have been interested in the poetry of Yeats since some unscholarly literary choices as a teenager led me to the view that Jilly Cooper's Declan O'Hara was a figure to be admired. Those of you with good memories or a penchant for rereading the books of your youth, or who have kept up with the brilliantly cast Disney+ series over the last years, will recall that the aforementioned Declan is the Irish TV presenter in *Rivals* who fights passionately for justice and exposes corruption (other passions and exposures are also available as is idiomatic in a Cooper production). He also explicitly identifies with Yeats and declaims his poetry loudly, extensively and, often, drunkenly. While I'm far from being an expert on the subject of Yeats, there are a handful of his poems that I know well and enjoy. In this one, I am particularly struck by that couplet at the end of the first stanza, and by the way in which the language creates a sense of menace – it's a clever trick and it is interesting to think about how he does it.

As well as leading the students into something difficult that is neither their native mental habitat nor mine, poetry allows us to think explicitly about how to use words. I need to be careful here – I am sure we can agree that using words is a skill that is enormously powerful in the grown-up world, and we know that children are taught a variety of kinds of writing at school: everyone takes GCSE English Language and there is no comparison between the complexity, breadth and nuance in the language used by a 16-year-old compared with that produced by their five-year-old self (and this is even true of the Molesworths of this world). In primary and early secondary school, students will be encouraged to write imaginatively and even as they hit the exam years their essays will receive feedback on how their choices and structures have affected the way their ideas have come across. A huge amount of thinking explicitly about words and word choices is part of the core curriculum but I sense that there is space to build further on these foundations. If you were to press me for specifics, I think I'd argue that the rhythms and cadences of students' writing can be something to which they do not attend, don't understand and don't recognise as an aspect of writing to care about.

The Second Coming is also a great topic for a session of the Cabinet of Curiosity because it provides a jumping-off point for such a wide range of ideas – it can be a starting point for understanding the Irish independence struggles of the early twentieth century, the Troubles of the late twentieth century (which intersects nicely with the British politics session) and even the current arrangements (which have been in the news in recent years as the UK tried to make its way through the Brexit quagmire). Why did Yeats think things were falling apart? What was the Irish War of Independence? Who are Sinn Féin? What was Home Rule? Why is this still an issue 100 years later? Are the differences fundamentally religious or is that incidental?

A similar question can be asked if the poem is allowed to take us into the Middle East. In 1919, there were tensions between Jewish and Arab communities, the 'solution' to which was a British mandate in the region. I don't know if Yeats was specifically thinking about this when he wrote (there was plenty going on closer to home), but there is here too a sense of things falling apart – in this case the Sykes–Picot Agreement which divided up the Ottoman territories and was rocked from its colonial slumber by the Turkish War of Independence.

Some of the students in my class will recognise the 'second coming' as something relevant to Christianity but I have students of all faiths and none in my classes and am faced with a challenge. I have tended to skirt round or skate over the theological significance of the poem: the language in the poem is so rich and the time so short that skimming over bits tends to be inevitable. However, for a confident teacher and an interested class there is a lot to talk about, from the descriptions of the beasts in Revelation to the prophecies that the Messiah would come in Bethlehem – alongside which we can wonder what the author had in mind: how much was Yeats making a religious or theological statement? I rather think that he would have had the theology in the back of his mind as he wrote rather than at the front. It seems that his own cosmology was rooted in the idea of circling years: ages or gyres that had their own coherence and caused disturbance as the world moved from one to the next.

The science of falconry and the Riddle of the Sphinx are diverting sidesteps (unless you have a passion for birds of prey or are a Classics scholar). The Sphinx story is particularly diverting as the Greek Sphinx and the Egyptian one are not closely related in time or mythology. That is possibly a session in its own right, as is poetic intertextuality: the way one poem influences another; the way one poet builds on the ideas and words already written. There is a programme on BBC Radio 4 called *Add to Playlist* in which Jeffrey Boakye and Cerys Matthews link together a chain of musical pieces using elements they have in common and I imagine world literature as a great three-dimensional version of this, with poets, writers and artists all reacting to and feeding off each other. While reading *The Second Coming*, for example, I have the sense that Shelley's *Ozymandias* has been looming off stage in the form of two vast and trunkless legs of stone standing in the desert. There's no direct quotation but it feels to me as though it's more than simply 'poems set in the desert' – a little googling and it turns out that other scholars have found this link (and also, apparently, one to *Prometheus Unbound*, which is a poem I don't know and therefore an idea that I'm even less qualified to speak upon than most of this chapter). Works inspired or illuminated by *The Second Coming* include Chinua Achebe's book *Things Fall Apart* (the first in a trilogy, the second of which also takes its title from a poem, this time by T.S. Eliot). Had we time, therefore, we could take a step into the colonial history of West Africa and possibly a diversion into yam farming (a key aspect of the plot of *Things Fall Apart*).

This session always feels as though I'm letting the brakes off and allowing the lesson to career along a road that I've not plotted. This is quite scary, but it is the spirit of the Cabinet of Curiosity (*Spiritus Arcae*?) that curiosity doesn't always take you where you think it's going to. One of the joys of asking questions is that you don't know what the answer is going to be and one of the problems with school curricula is that most of the time we need to take students to a specific destination; we have to teach them what they need for their exams. The Cabinet has no exams, it has no destination, it has no bounds, and being able to feel this as freedom rather than anarchy is our goal in running the course in the first place.

Chapter 7
Quantum chromodynamics (Or how to bite off more than you can chew and not choke)

We've done politics, art, poetry – it must be time for some science and to go looking for the mysteries that lie at the centre of the atom. Atoms are very small, which means that they're easy to bring to class (it's actually unavoidable), but difficult to study: a million, million, million hydrogen atoms weigh just a millionth of a gram and no microscope is going to help you look inside. Making sense of what's going on in there is no small task but I'm not one to balk at a challenge, so here goes. After all, what could be more curious than the world of quantum physics where we explain the behaviour of colourless particles by referring to their colour?

You may have been taught a 'solar system' model of the atom – the nucleus is a dense collection of protons (positively charged) and neutrons (neutral), while whizzing around it, in a series of increasingly large 'orbitals', are the light and negatively charged electrons. I sat in a science lesson once while the teacher explained that this couldn't be an accurate model because when charged particles move through an electric field (as the electrons are doing in this 'solar system'), they give off gamma rays and lose energy. Eventually they would crash into the nucleus and we know that doesn't happen (in fact, chemistry relies on it not happening).

This is a good example of science refining its models of reality as more information becomes available, but it wasn't my primary concern as I looked at the picture in front of me; the explanation of shells rather than orbitals, and probability wave forms rather than moving particles, did

Chapter 7 Quantum chromodynamics

nothing to alleviate my sense of unease. My problem, you see, was with the nucleus, in which a group of protons was, apparently happily, hobnobbing with a collection of neutrons.

We are taught that like charges repel – this is because of the electrostatic force, generated by stationary charged particles such as the protons in the diagram below. Opposite charges attract, but there are none of those in the nucleus and so, according to my understanding at the time, all nuclei larger than hydrogen (which only has one proton and therefore doesn't have to worry about this) should blow themselves apart in a way we are confident they haven't so far and are hoping they won't start to when they get this particular memo.

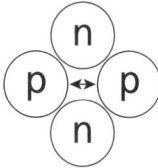

A nucleus (helium) with two protons and two neutrons, showing the repulsive electrostatic force

In order to explain the observed phenomenon of there being atoms with more than one proton, we need to postulate an attractive force inside a larger nucleus. If we were listening to Ringo Starr while we were thinking about this problem, and therefore had octopuses (or octopodes, either is fine) on the brain, we might think about a tentacular creature reaching out for each proton and holding them together. Bar magnets having a more tangible reality than protons, and being subject to the same repulsive force, we might draw something like this:

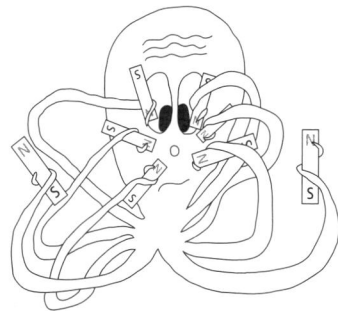

The postulated Subatomic Octopus attempting to resist eight electrostatic forces

Fortunately for those of us who find it difficult to believe in this explanation, the physicists are there already. Rather than our tiny cephalopod straining to hold the north poles of the bar magnets together, there is a 'strong' nuclear force which holds nuclei together through a process called quantum chromodynamics. In order to begin to understand what is going on, we need to be clear about a few basics.

1 The model of the universe has everything being made up of fundamental particles – some of which are responsible for matter and some for the forces experienced by the matter.

2 Every matter particle has its own antiparticle, including some particles, such as photons, that are their own antiparticle.

3 Einstein tells us that $E = mc^2$, which means that energy and mass are interchangeable. This is not just a great catchphrase but is true in two ways – first, a particle and antiparticle, when they meet, will annihilate into a burst of energy, and second, a particle and antiparticle pair can spontaneously blink into existence using up some of the energy available in the universe. We must imagine all space filled with ambient energy and thus with a soup of particle/antiparticle pairs that blink into existence, enjoy each other's company briefly and then annihilate, returning the energy to the pot.

4 Forces are difficult to understand (especially attractive ones) and the simplest explanation I've come across is that they are a redistribution of particles that moves the universe into a more favourable state. For our purposes, we simply need to know that for there to be a force between two particles, there has to be a transfer of energy and for that, a particle of some kind has to move from one to the other.

5 Protons and neutrons are not fundamental particles. They are made up of sub-particles called 'quarks'. Quarks have two important properties: colours (the 'chromo' in chromodynamics) and flavours. The possible colours for quarks are red, blue and green and there are six possible flavours, although today we will only be considering up and down. GCSE physics reminds us that red, blue and green are the primary colours of light and that when mixed they give white. This is an important feature of quantum chromodynamics: coloured particles cannot exist on their own or escape into the wild – they always group together to make white. Antiquarks have the same flavours but opposite colours: anti-red is cyan, anti-blue is yellow and anti-green is magenta.

6 Bosons are the particles that carry force by moving energy from one particle to another (see point 4). This family of particles includes photons

Chapter 7 Quantum chromodynamics

and gluons. Photons carry the electromagnetic force which, with the aid of a little diagram, enables us to explain how protons repel each other:

A Feynman diagram showing a photon (wavy line) moving between two protons (p) – the exchange of particles is a force

The diagram was invented by Richard Feynman to explain to those with less scientific intuition (which, at the last count, was everybody) how forces work and shows two protons, p_1 and p_2, approaching each other from the bottom of the diagram, getting too close for comfort, exchanging a photon and then heading off in a new direction.

Gluons are another type of boson and they carry the strong nuclear force. This is more complicated than the electromagnetic force and will occupy us for the rest of the session. Each gluon has a colour and an anti-colour that do not add up to white (they can, for example, be red/anti-blue). When a gluon interacts with a quark, the colours get combined in a way that is almost exactly the opposite of how mixing paints worked at primary school. Welcome to the zany, upside-down world of subatomic physics.

Having met gluons and taken Einstein in our stride, we're now in a position to look inside a proton, where we find one down and two up quarks. We don't need to worry about charges for what we're doing, and part of me regrets even mentioning it, but for completeness I feel I should tell you that up quarks have a charge of +⅔ each and each down quark has a charge of –⅓. A little imagination and calculation will suggest that a neutron should be made of one up and two down quarks, while a proton is two up quarks and one down. This is, indeed, the case.

We do need to worry about colours and inside either a neutron or a proton one quark will be blue, one red and one green; it doesn't matter which is which.

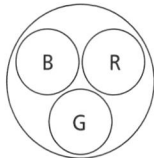

A proton with one down and two up quarks. For our purposes it doesn't matter which is which, but for the sake of keeping track, the one at the bottom is down

The first thing the strong nuclear force does is to hold these quarks together. According to rule 4, a particle needs to be able to move from one to another and, according to rule 6, we are expecting it to be a boson – in particular, a gluon. To follow how this works we need to understand the maths of coloured light. Essentially, white light counts as zero (so blue plus white is blue); anything plus its anti-colour gives white (for example, red plus cyan); red plus blue plus green is white; and whatever we do must conserve the colours we have. Because gluons have a colour and an anti-colour, they can appear out of nowhere (using rule 3) and disappear similarly.

Let's see this in action, starting with a blue up quark. The colour of the quark is, in some ways, like a suit of clothes that it can put on and take off subject to a couple of rules. First, we can't have naked (or colourless) quarks – atoms are prudish in that way; second, the colour arithmetic has to stay the same – colours cannot be created or destroyed. So, if the blue quark wants to become a red quark then it needs to get the redness from somewhere and pass on the blueness (of course, subatomic particles don't have volition, they don't 'want' things, and the scientific explanation for such changes is that they put the universe in an energetically more favourable state). The way it does this is to create a gluon (which has a small amount of mass and therefore requires the quark to take a bit of energy from the universe – which it does by invoking rule 3). The gluon will have a colour and an anti-colour, and in this case it will have the colour blue (which it gets from the quark) and the anti-colour cyan (which it gets by giving red to the quark because cyan is anti-red). The colour maths now adds up: blue = red + cyan + blue and Einstein takes care of the energy/mass equation for us. Check that you understand this now: this is not going to become less impenetrable.

We will watch this happening in the proton above and follow through with a particle exchange that leads to a force holding the proton together. This is the proton after the blue quark has undressed:

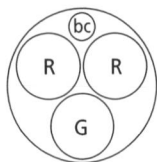

The blue quark (B) has turned into a red quark (R) together with a blue/cyan gluon (bc)

Chapter 7 Quantum chromodynamics

Now the blue/cyan gluon and the right-hand red quark can combine to make a blue quark (because blue + cyan + red = blue). This puts us back in the original position but with the colours of the red and blue quarks swapped over. A particle has been exchanged and so we can have a force (in this case attractive, holding the proton together).

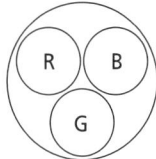

The blue/cyan gluon (bc) has merged with the top-right red quark (R) to make a blue quark (B)

Unfortunately for us, gluons can't move from one proton to another (because their colours don't add up to white) and so we need to build on our model. We can do that by allowing a gluon to turn spontaneously into a quark/anti-quark pair using rule 3 and colouring them using its colour/anti-colour pair. We still don't really care about the flavour of the quarks, but when this happens the quark and anti-quark have the same flavour (up/anti-up or down/anti-down).

Going back to the middle of our three diagrams above, this looks like this (you'll notice that the quark and anti-quark look the same – as far as we're concerned, you can think of an anti-quark just as a quark that has an anti-colour):

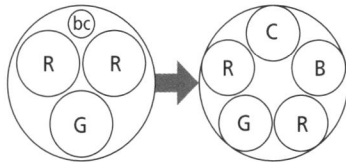

A gluon is turned into a quark/anti-quark pair

Now, the red and cyan quark/anti-quark pair can form a particle called a meson which, since red + cyan = white, can escape the proton and set off on a journey to find another one. They could also annihilate themselves into a burst of energy (not even giving off a gluon, since their colours cancel out) and this is the very frequent but rather boring fate of such particles. We remain focused on those enterprising few who head into the unknown.

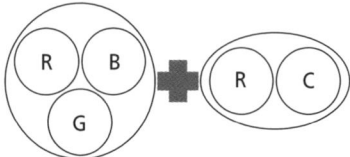

The formation of an enterprising meson

When it gets there, the process can be reversed: the meson enters the new proton and a quark/anti-quark pair annihilate, creating a gluon which combines with one of the remaining quarks to change its colour. A particle has been transferred and so we get a force – again an attractive one.

One point here is that mesons are relatively heavy (a back of the envelope calculation gives two-thirds the mass of a proton – it's actually more complicated than this, but it will do for our purposes) and unstable (the quark/anti-quark pair is very excited by the possibility of annihilation). This means that the strong nuclear force has a very short range of operation; in contrast, the electromagnetic force, transmitted by the massless and indestructible photon, operates over a potentially infinite distance.

Another point is that while this explains why we can have atoms that are larger than hydrogen (which is great news for all us carbon-based life forms), and even predicts that the more protons you have the more neutrons you'll need (because proton–proton gives an attractive strong nuclear force and a repulsive electromagnetic force but proton–neutron gives just the attractive force), it doesn't explain why you can't just add neutrons to an atom to make it more and more stable (you can't – most elements have a sweet spot for the number of neutrons and above that they become unstable). In order to explain that we would need to add the weak nuclear force to our model which, not being quantum chromodynamics, is beyond the scope of this chapter.

Rationale and reflections

With this session, more than any of the others, it feels like we're not just branching out sideways into things students could be interested in, but diving vertically into ideas that, for some of them, will turn up in their studies in a couple of years. Generally, I lean into universal accessibility and try to avoid any prerequisite understanding for the sessions. After all, there are plenty of sideways options to branch into: students are studying a maximum of four academic subjects out of the dozens available at sixth form but, more than that, they are studying syllabi that are carefully limited and therefore consist of just a thin slice of the subject they represent.

This session, however, fulfils a couple of important purposes that, to my mind at least, justify the mystified and occasionally desperate looks I get from students when I try to persuade them of the existence of the subatomic octopus. The first key message, I hope, is that curiosity is fine, that students should challenge what they're taught, should think hard about new information and test it for sense. It's clear to all concerned that my imaginary cephalopod is straining every sinew to hold the like poles of the magnets together and GCSE physics teaches us clearly that electrical forces work the same way, with like charges repelling each other (which is unsurprising as the photon is the carrier particle for the electromagnetic force). Am I suggesting that GCSE classrooms should be filled with students protesting against the apparent nonsense of the nucleus? Well, I think it might be an indicator of a healthy level of curiosity, but I'm not actually campaigning for it and if you, dear reader, are a GCSE physics student, please don't make your teacher's life more difficult by going to class with a 'Free the Proton' placard. But, and it's a big but, I think there should be hands up asking questions about how the nucleus holds together and that teachers should have to say, 'Good point – there's an attractive force that's stronger than the repulsion. It's called the strong nuclear force and you can either wait four years until it comes up in your undergraduate physics course or you can come and see me after school and I'll wave my hands around and try to give you the basics.' The Cabinet of Curiosity is about finding fascination in the world, about the delight that comes from learning for its own sake, but it's also about interrogating our sources, about not being blindly accepting of all we're told, of expecting our model of the world to make sense.

The second key idea here is that science is fun and about asking questions and expecting satisfying answers. Sixth-formers often identify as STEM and non-STEM types and I am keen to persuade them that this is an artificial and unhelpful distinction. Normally this consists of me, a devoted mathematician, quoting poetry and being fascinated by great art, but I think we (I) also need to show those who have ditched science at the earliest opportunity that there are still joys to be had; that it's not a mysterious world that only a special kind of person can understand, but a set of facts and ideas that they have chosen to deprioritise in their learning journey.

Sometimes I think, as I'm delivering this session, that I have bitten off more than I can chew. With the topology in session one I'm on home ground – I'm confident that I'm not going to be teaching them anything false; with the Stone Age there's a great deal of 'actually nobody really knows' and if I'm not up to date with latest findings then at least those findings are coming in fast enough that even the latest ones are never going to be the full story; the British politics in chapter 4 is idiosyncratic and any mistakes can easily be covered by the misremembering of a child; and both art and poetry place a strong emphasis on personal response and interpretation – the way I see or read something doesn't claim to be objectively true and I am confident that I know enough, have thought hard enough, that my ideas will have value to the students in the class as they put together their own response. Physics, however, is different. It doesn't make the same claims to objective truth that maths does – simply that it's the best explanation we have for the observed universe. Physics doesn't claim to be right, but it does know when you are wrong – if your description doesn't fit with observations (and really, the subatomic octopus doesn't come close) then it's wrong. This means I have had to be more careful and to stick closer to the script with this session than others – I am also ready to answer questions or challenges with, 'I don't know – let's both look it up and reconvene when we have more answers between us.' This is uncomfortable, but it is at the heart of the Cabinet and I think that it's good to lean into the idea of the teacher as non-expert occasionally – I'm pretty confident that I know more than the class does about this (I'm way more worried that one day I'll get caught out on art or poetry – a Year 12 Turner buff could easily know more than me, whereas it's quite unusual for them to go through A-level physics and out the far side in advance of actually taking any A-levels), but that doesn't mean I have to know everything.

Chapter 8
American politics, history and government
(Or the joy of reacting to current affairs)

One year in every four, the machinery of American government hits the news as the country goes through the process of deciding the next president and so, one year in every four, it feels appropriate to explain how the US Constitution works and, as far as it's possible, why. More than one year in every four, however, the USA makes the news for one reason or another – it is so large, so powerful and recently so, erm, let's say dynamic, that there's often some element in its history and politics that's worth covering. I therefore have a session that explains how the history of the USA shaped its constitution and how that constitution underpins the politics we see in the news.

We start in 1787 when Delaware was the first state to join the Union, creating the perplexing situation of a union of one. Fortunately for Delaware, this is an entirely technical issue – the 13 North American British colonies had become states in 1776 on the Declaration of Independence and they had already united in 1777 under the Articles of Confederation (under which they fought the War of Independence with, some would say, no little success). Delaware's 1787 initiative was in ratifying the Constitution that is still in use (somewhat amended) today, and it was followed by Pennsylvania, New Jersey, Georgia, Connecticut, Massachusetts, Maryland, South Carolina and New Hampshire in that order. Article 7 of the Constitution sets out that should nine states ratify it then it will come into effect for those states. At this point, therefore, the new document kicked in, although the country it created was not really viable until the two richest states, Virginia and New York, joined. A start date of 4 March 1789 was set (time being required for the first set of elections under the new rules) and both of these states ratified the Constitution before this (although New York failed to get itself organised to have elections in time), leaving just two of the original 13 colonies: North Carolina, which signed up once the Bill of Rights had been added, and Rhode Island, which had initially voted in a referendum against the new constitution but now found itself in danger of being a tiny foreign country surrounded by a superpower. This not being an attractive proposition, Rhode Island bowed to the inevitable and signed up too.

The Constitution sets out three elections to take place: for the House of Representatives, the Senate and the position of president. Article 1 Section 2 of the Constitution sets out in fairly impenetrable style how the House will be elected:

The House of Representatives shall be composed of Members chosen every second Year by the People of the several States, and the Electors in each State shall have the Qualifications requisite for Electors of the most numerous Branch of the State Legislature. ... The Number of Representatives shall not exceed one for every thirty Thousand, but each State shall have at Least one Representative; and until such enumeration shall be made, the State of New Hampshire shall be entitled to chuse three, Massachusetts eight, Rhode-Island and Providence Plantations one, Connecticut five, New-York six, New Jersey four, Pennsylvania eight, Delaware one, Maryland six, Virginia ten, North Carolina five, South Carolina five, and Georgia three.

The key ideas here are that the members of the House of Representatives are elected every two years, that every state gets at least one seat and that the number of seats depends on the population of the state. The states are divided into districts, each of which elects one person to Congress (the legislative branch of government, composed of the House of Representatives and the Senate), with the number of districts being chosen to match the number of representatives the state is entitled to. The corresponding text for the Senate (Article 1 Section 3) is rather more straightforward:

The Senate of the United States shall be composed of two Senators from each State, chosen by the Legislature thereof, for six Years; and each Senator shall have one Vote.

The oddity here is that the senators are chosen by the state legislature rather than directly elected – which means we have to briefly dip into local government. The federal nature of the United States means that each state is, in origin, an independently governed territory that concedes some independence to the centre in exchange for greater strength and security. Each state therefore has its own government elected by its own constituents and this government remains much stronger than local councils in the UK (it's more like the independent parliaments in Scotland, Wales and Northern Ireland). Originally, the state parliament (legislature) would choose two appropriately serious citizens to represent it in the US Senate. This changed when the 17th Amendment to the Constitution was passed in 1913. Since then, senators have been elected by direct popular vote within each state.

Amendments have been part of the Constitution from its beginning – Article 5 sets out the mechanism for making changes and requires two-thirds of both the House of Representatives and the Senate to agree that it is necessary, and then three-quarters of the states to ratify the change. James Madison (who would later become the fourth president), writing in the Federalist Papers in 1788, said, 'It guards equally against that extreme facility which would render the Constitution too mutable; and that extreme difficulty which might perpetuate its discovered faults.' The first ten amendments form the Bill of Rights and were proposed together by the first Congress in 1789. Seventeen further amendments (including the 17th) have been passed since then, with the most recent becoming law in 1992.

So much for the legislature. What about the executive? Article 2 Section 1 sets out a procedure for selecting a group of electors (called the Electoral College) that will choose the president:

Each State shall appoint, in such Manner as the Legislature thereof may direct, a Number of Electors, equal to the whole Number of Senators and Representatives to which the State may be entitled in the Congress ...

The states are entitled to choose how the electors are chosen; once chosen, the electors come together in an Electoral College to make the decision on which candidate should become president. Since the 1820s, the decision is simply made by popular vote of the electors and in most states it's a winner-takes-all affair, with voters making their choice for the presidential candidate and the winner taking all that state's electors. The electors are real people and each state elects a number as specified by the Constitution – they're not politicians who go to hustings and campaign for votes but shadowy figures chosen by the presidential candidates and the political parties behind them. There are a couple of oddities to be aware of here: the first is that in Maine and Nebraska it isn't winner-takes-all: the statewide vote only selects two electors (which you can think of as the two for the Senate) – the remaining electors (one for each representative) are chosen by the vote in each congressional district (the subdivisions of the state that are used to elect the representatives to the House). This means that while in the other states the most popular candidate (across the state) gets all the electors, in these two states they can be split if one part of the state (district) is more left- or right-leaning than the rest. The second wrinkle is that there's no constitutional requirement for the electors to vote for the candidate they were chosen to side with and historically there have been many instances of 'faithless' electors who were chosen to vote for one candidate but changed their allegiance. (In 2016, for example, Hillary Clinton won the presidential vote in Hawaii from Donald Trump but one of her electors voted for Bernie Sanders when it came to the crunch.) The number of such electors varies wildly – in 2012, for example, there were none while in 2016 there were ten. Some states have passed laws to eliminate this wrinkle and to ensure the Electoral College vote goes the way the people voted for.

In the first election, in 1788 (and 1789 – this is the only election to have run across two years), ten states voted (New York hadn't got its act together in time and North Carolina and Rhode Island were still considering the Constitution) and all the presidential votes went to George Washington. Virginia had the most electors with 12 and Delaware the fewest with three. The 1792 election was similarly straightforward, with Washington the only presidential candidate to receive Electoral College votes. By this time there were 15 states (Vermont had become the 14th and Kentucky the 15th), and Virginia now had 21 electors.

The early presidential elections may have been a foregone conclusion but the elections to Congress were not. There were no political parties at this point but there were politicians who broadly supported the government and those who didn't (you can see how this would lead to a two-party system soon enough). In 1792, in the Senate, the administration held onto a 16–14 majority, but the anti-administration group gained a 54–51 majority in the House of Representatives.

The number of seats given to each state (and hence the number of electors) had been reapportioned following the first census and was therefore not governed by the temporary arrangement we looked at earlier. The Constitution sets out the need for and operation of censuses in Article 1 Section 2:

Representatives and direct Taxes shall be apportioned among the several States which may be included within this Union, according to their respective Numbers, which shall be determined by adding to the whole Number of free Persons, including those bound to Service for a Term of Years, and excluding Indians not taxed, three fifths of all other Persons. The actual enumeration shall be made within three Years after the first Meeting of the Congress of the United States, and within every subsequent Term of ten Years, in such Manner as they shall by Law direct.

The first thing to note here is that as well as not counting 'Indians not taxed', the Constitution explicitly counts free persons and three-fifths of all other persons. This clause is called the Three-fifths Compromise and was put into the Constitution to balance the conflicting requirements of slave states and free states. The argument of the slave states was that they should get representation based on the people who lived there. The argument of the free states was that since enslaved people couldn't vote, their owners shouldn't get additional representation for owning them. Three-fifths was a rather murky in-between and was explicitly repealed by the 14th Amendment of 1868, which specified that all male citizens over the age of 21 should be allowed to vote and that the total of all persons (still not including Indians untaxed) should be used to assign representation.

The second point is that assigning representatives fairly is a non-trivial operation mathematically. This might seem strange: you would expect that once you have decided on a total number of representatives and counted the number of people in each state, you could simply use fractions to get the proportions right. Pause for one moment and think about what 'simply use fractions' means – we might imagine the joys of slicing politicians into smaller pieces but it's hardly a basis for sound government. We have to have a whole number of representatives from each state, which means we have to have a system for rounding fractions up or down. The trouble is that any algorithmic way of doing this has the potential to create apparently paradoxical (and therefore definitely undesirable) situations. The maths of this is a session in itself so we excuse ourselves, leaving those who are interested to look up the 'Alabama paradox'.

It is, incidentally, the 14th Amendment (section 3) that makes anyone ineligible to serve as president (or a range of other offices) who is found guilty of engaging in or aiding insurrection against the state.

The first competitive presidential election was in 1796 after George Washington decided that two terms was enough. This view was shared by all subsequent presidents up to Franklin D. Roosevelt, who decided in 1940 that he should run for a third and, in 1944, a fourth term. In 1947, the 22nd Amendment was passed to prevent a president who had been elected twice from running for a third term. The 1796 election was also the first one fought with political parties. The eras of American politics are divided up by 'party systems' – the first one being the Federalists (generally northeastern and, in 1796, represented by John Adams) against the Democratic Republicans (generally southern and represented by Thomas Jefferson). Tennessee had been added as a 16th state in the summer of 1796 and, like Delaware, had just three electors.

Adams won the election and Jefferson, with the second-most votes, became the vice president. This was according to Article 2 Section 1 of the Constitution, which gave each elector two votes to cast as they saw fit – the candidate with the most votes becoming president and the one in second place becoming vice president. This was resolved by the 12th Amendment in 1803, which separated out the election of vice president from that of president and gave each elector one vote in each election. Before then, however, it caused difficulty for John Adams who had a vice president he couldn't work with. (It was particularly difficult when, in the Napoleonic Wars, Adams sided with Britain and Jefferson with France.) It also led to the situation in 1800 where Jefferson and Aaron Burr had run together as a joint ticket but the Democratic Republican electors couldn't decide among themselves how to arrange it that Burr got fewer votes than Jefferson (with 71) but still more than the Federalist candidate (Adams again, who got 68). As a result, there was a tie for president and the House of Representatives fulfilled its constitutional duty as set out in Article 2 Section 1:

> ... *The Person having the greatest Number of Votes shall be the President, if such Number be a Majority of the whole Number of Electors appointed; and if there be more than one who have such Majority, and have an equal Number of Votes, then the House of Representatives shall immediately chuse by Ballot one of them for President; and if no Person have a Majority, then from the five highest on the List the said House shall in like Manner chuse the President. But in chusing the President, the Votes shall be taken by States, the*

Representation from each State having one Vote; A quorum for this Purpose shall consist of a Member or Members from two thirds of the States, and a Majority of all the States shall be necessary to a Choice. ...

In brief, the representatives from each state have to cast one vote between them and the candidate with the most votes becomes president. As a fallback for the rare case of a tie, this must have seemed a good solution to the Founding Fathers, who had no experience of political parties and may have been hoping that, in times of difficulty, the wisdom of serious men would coalesce around making the best choice for the country. In 1800, however, there were eight states that favoured the Federalists and eight where the Democratic Republicans had the majority. The two candidates with the most votes were Jefferson and Burr, both Democratic Republicans, whose states conscientiously voted for Jefferson as had been agreed beforehand. Meanwhile, the Federalist states saw an opportunity to cause trouble and decided to vote for Burr to become president, not because (as far as I can tell) they preferred his policies, but because it would have been funny. This meant that there was a tie, with eight states on each side, which took 36 votes and the intervention of Alexander Hamilton to resolve, after which Thomas Jefferson became the third president.

Alexander Hamilton's involvement with the early United States is the subject of a musical in which he is described as 'The ten dollar founding father without a father' – a tribute both to his difficult childhood and to his portrait featuring on the ten-dollar bill. This is a rather incongruous inclusion – in the sequence Washington, Jefferson, Lincoln, Hamilton, Jackson, Grant on the $1, $2, $5, $10, $20 and $50 bank notes, he is the only non-president. (I'm assured that Benjamin Franklin, also never president, appears on the $100 note but I've never actually owned one myself.) There was some talk of replacing Hamilton and some optimism that there might finally be a woman recognised on American currency but this was scotched by the success of the musical and subsequent adoration of the scrappy and hungry young man who got a lot farther by working a lot harder.

Back to the nineteenth century and the second party system, which began in about 1828. The term 'party system' is used by scholars of American politics to cover periods of time when key issues of policy and geography divide the political parties and allows them to group elections in which there are similar voting patterns across the country. In the early nineteenth century, this involved the creation or dissipation of new parties and there is always a merging period rather than a definitive date for the change from one party system to another, as one party declines in popularity or coherence and new ones arise from the splits or in the vacuum left behind. The election in 1828 was between John Quincy Adams (son of John Adams) of the National Republican Party (which was in decline and would soon be replaced by the Whig Party) and Andrew Jackson of the Democratic Party (a party formed following the 1824 election which, like the election of 1800, had ended with the House of Representatives having to resolve an inconclusive result as there were four candidates (all ostensibly from the Democratic Republican Party) receiving substantial numbers of electoral votes and no one candidate receiving a majority). Quincy Adams had won the run-off in 1824 with Jackson second, but the 1828 rematch was a conclusive victory for Jackson and the Democrats. By 1828, there were 24 states, with Ohio (17), Louisiana (18), Indiana (19), Mississippi (20), Illinois (21), Alabama (22), Maine (23) and Missouri (24) having joined the Union. New York was now the largest single state with 36 Electoral College votes and Delaware was still joint smallest with three, alongside Mississippi, Missouri and Illinois.

The accession of Maine and Missouri in 1821 was the result of the Missouri Compromise, under which Maine seceded from Massachusetts (from which it had always been geographically distinct) as a free state, Missouri became a slave state and any future states could only allow slavery if they were south of Missouri's southern border. The Three-fifths Compromise had guaranteed enough representation for the slave states and a careful alternation in the addition of new states between northern ones (Ohio, Indiana, Illinois) and southern ones (Louisiana, Mississippi, Alabama) had kept this balance but the expansion westwards caused the tensions to bubble up. Two further compromises were attempted as the nation hurtled, apparently inevitably, towards civil war.

The Compromise of 1850 allowed the entrance of California as a free state (despite being, in part, further south than Missouri), fixed the northern borders of Texas and included the Fugitive Slave Act, which mandated that all citizens and governments of free states had to co-operate with returning runaway enslaved people to their owners. Then, in 1854, the Kansas–Nebraska Act repealed the earlier Missouri Compromise for the Kansas and Nebraska territories and put their status as slave or free states in the hands of popular sovereignty (thus giving them the chance of becoming slave states when, under the previous law, they would have to have been free).

In the 1856 election, the main opposition to the Democrats (led by James Buchanan) were the Republicans (despite the valiant efforts of the xenophobic, anti-Catholic and amusingly named Know-Nothing Party), whose candidate was John Frémont. There were now 31 states, the Union having been joined by Arkansas, Michigan, Florida, Texas, Iowa, Wisconsin and California. New York was still the largest state with 35 votes and eternal minnow Delaware was joined by Florida on three. The main issues of the election were slavery, the preservation of the Union and, particularly, the civil disturbances that were taking place in Kansas. The Republicans said that the expansion of slavery undermined the foundations on which the Union had been built, the Democrats said that a Republican president would lead to the secession of southern states and both parties supported the Kansas–Nebraska Act and blamed the other for the violence that had ensued. The Know-Nothing Party said that Frémont was a Catholic, which he wasn't. Buchanan won with 174 electoral votes to Frémont's 114 and Millard Fillmore of the Know-Nothings won Maryland's eight votes. Fillmore deserves rather better than to be this footnote to the 1856 election, having previously served as vice president and as the Whig Party's last president (and thus the most recent not to have been either Democrat or Republican). Any history that seeks to do justice to every character is doomed to both failure and excessive length and so the Fillmorites among my readers will have to fume quietly as we wade into the American Civil War.

Bleeding Kansas is the name given to a long-running campaign of violence designed to sway any vote on the status of the territory as a slave or free state. Between 1855 and 1861, Kansas was in a state of civil war with two separate capitals, two constitutions and armed attacks from one side to the other during which time two other states, Minnesota and Oregon, became free states. In total, about 200 people were killed in Kansas as the slavery debate brought new meaning to popular sovereignty. In 1861, Abraham Lincoln (of the Republican Party) became president and seven southern states seceded from the Union. That left Congress with the votes required to admit Kansas as a free state, resolving this particular problem while kicking off the, admittedly much larger, one of the American Civil War.

This conflict left over half a million American soldiers dead, saw West Virginia become a state separate from Virginia, saw Nevada join the Union as a new state and resolved the slave/free debate via the 13th Amendment, which abolished slavery. The 14th and 15th Amendments were also approved during this period and secured the rights of all Americans irrespective of race, colour or previous servitude. This paragraph is obviously an inadequate summary of the American Civil War, which might justify an entire chapter of its own, but must be sadly abandoned like Robert Frost's slightly more-travelled road, which he left for another day.

Ever since the Civil War, the two parties have been Democrat and Republican but exactly what these terms mean in terms of policy and geography has changed (and these changes have been what has delineated the subsequent party systems). From the end of the war there was a period in which the south and east tended to vote Democrat and the north and west Republican, with the line approximating to the border between the slave and free states – some wounds take a long time to heal. The fortunes of the two parties fluctuated during this time but the broad pattern under the fourth and fifth party systems was similar and so the political maps of 1880 and 1960 have very similar appearances. In 1880, Republican James Garfield and Democrat Winfield Hancock both won 19 states and were within 2000 overall votes of each other (the closest election ever by this measure), but Garfield gained a convincing 214–155 Electoral College victory. Between the end of the Civil War and this election, two states, Nebraska then Colorado, had joined, but New York was still the most important with 35 votes, and five states (including Delaware) had just three.

By 1960, the states had reached the current total of 50: North Dakota, South Dakota, Montana, Washington, Idaho and Wyoming all became states (in that order) within an 8-month period in 1889 and 1890; Utah was admitted in 1896 once it abandoned its plans for polygamy (which had been a key part of the Mormon settlement there, but was antithetical to the rest of the USA); Oklahoma's story is one of betrayal of the Native American tribes who had been forcibly settled to the area in the nineteenth century but had their land taken by the federal government in order for the area to become the 46th state in 1907. The year 1912 saw New Mexico and Arizona join in January and February respectively, and in 1959, either side of Buddy Holly's death, Alaska and Hawaii became states. New York still had the most electoral votes, with 45, and Alaska, Delaware, Hawaii, Nevada and Vermont had three each.

The 1960 presidential election was between John F. Kennedy (Democrat) and Richard Nixon (Republican). The key issue was the Cold War, with Kennedy claiming that the Republican administration (in which Nixon had been the vice president) had allowed the country to fall behind economically, while Nixon said that his experience was necessary to stand up to the Soviet Union. It was almost as tight an election as 1880, with Kennedy gaining fewer states and winning the popular vote by just 0.17% (about 100,000 votes). Due to the electoral value of large states such as New York and Texas (both of which voted for him), Kennedy won a convincing electoral majority of 303 to 219. As well as the south and east, Kennedy won the industrial states of Illinois, Michigan and Minnesota while Nixon picked up Florida, Virginia and the northeast corner of Maine, Vermont and New Hampshire, as well as most of the west. Nixon's loss has been put down to his performance in the first-ever televised debates in which Kennedy's looks are thought to have helped him, but may equally be due to dubious campaigning decisions such as spending the weekend before the election trying to shore up Alaska's three votes while Kennedy was in New Jersey, Ohio, Michigan and Pennsylvania (combined 93 votes).

One interesting aspect of the 1960 election that ties it to 1880 and, in fact, further back in America's history, was that one Republican and 14 Democratic electors decided not to back their party's candidate, instead going for Harry Byrd who stood for segregationists who opposed voting rights for African Americans (which had been guaranteed for the last 90 years by the 15th Amendment). It was also the last election before the 23rd Amendment gave the District of Columbia three electoral votes as though it were a state, which it isn't. Article 1 Section 8 of the Constitution gave Congress authority over a capital district (if any states could be persuaded to give up the land); James Madison (in the Federalist Papers) said that the government needed land of its own for the purposes of security and independence; and the Compromise of 1790 (known to friends of Hamilton as 'the room where it happened') placed the capital on the border of Virginia and Maryland (rather than the more natural New York or Philadelphia) in exchange for a larger federal government with responsibility for a national debt.

Following the 1960 election there was a de-alignment period in which the Republican Party went after the socially conservative south and went through a period of dominance only punctuated by the 1976 election following Nixon's resignation as a result of the Watergate affair. Nixon won in 1972 by a margin of 520–17 electoral votes (George McGovern for the Democrats picked up only Massachusetts and Washington DC) and Ronald Reagan defeated Jimmy Carter in 1980 by 489–49, but the most one-sided election (and the largest number of electoral votes ever given to a presidential candidate) was in 1984 when Walter Mondale for the Democrats won only Minnesota and the ever-loyal DC, and Reagan won by 525–13.

Since then, the elections have been closer and since at least 2000 we have been in the sixth party system under which the Democrats have won in the northeast and west coast and the Republicans in the south, Midwest and mountain states. During this time the battlegrounds have shifted from Florida and New Mexico in 2000 (actually this election was phenomenally close, with five states decided by less than 1%) to Wisconsin and Pennsylvania in 2020.

The 2024 election was fought between Democrat Kamala Harris (sitting vice president) and Republican Donald Trump (president from 2017–2021) and the key issues were the economy, health care and concerns about the democratic process. This was the first presidential election to take place after the 2020 census, as a result of which California still had the largest electoral vote with 54, despite losing one for the first time in its history, and six states (still including Delaware) had three. The closest states were identified in advance as being the 'Rust Belt' of Wisconsin, Michigan and Pennsylvania – three states that had been industrial heartlands but which have been less prosperous as America moves from large-scale primary and secondary industries towards a high-tech and service economy – and Arizona, Georgia, Nevada and North Carolina, the contrastingly named 'Sun Belt'. Trump ended up winning all seven states; Wisconsin was the closest with a margin of 0.87%, and all except Arizona were within 5%.

Rationale and reflections

In a course designed to provoke curiosity, it's great to be able to respond to curiosity that the students bring with them and elections, British and American, have the power to break through into the teenage consciousness. This reasoning has led me to put together a separate explainer session on Ukraine and the war there in response to a discussion in which it became clear that this was a topic of much interest and little knowledge. There could be a whole course of explainers on global conflicts we know about (and some we don't), but I haven't yet written that one. Tell your friends about this book and maybe I'll get onto it.

American politics obligingly comes into the news every two to four years, which means that the slides get reused fairly frequently. The political history is also rather satisfying because there are answers to questions of 'Why is it like this?' whereas in the UK things tend to be more complex, less thought through, and more rooted in ancient tradition. The musical *Hamilton* has brought enough of an awareness of the Founding Fathers that there's something to build on, even if a smaller proportion of students have seen it than I think it deserves.

I am convinced that the compromises at the heart of the American Constitution (I've mentioned the Three-fifths Compromise, the 'room where it happened' and the Missouri Compromise, among others) say something important about politics. I'm also interested in the self-aware way in which the country has developed, that the Constitution was not just written but narrated (in the Federalist Papers) by statesmen who knew they also had to be politicians. Together, these reveal a complex, nuanced and messy truth about politics that is particularly important to explain to a generation that has grown up on soundbites and single-issue elections.

I'd like to persuade students that a good democracy is one where everybody's voice is heard and protected, rather than one where you (or anyone else) get exactly what you want. I'm not sure I've quite found the way of delivering this completely convincingly; perhaps, with it being politics, there is no way to deliver an idea completely convincingly, and it is against the style of the Cabinet of Curiosity for me to hammer my own views. I think it's also important sometimes to deliberately back away from being completely convincing in order to provide a well-reasoned counter-argument and leave the students to work their own way through the complexity, to question and be curious, to wonder what is really going on and why, and to go away pondering the question of where they personally stand.

Complexity is something that traditional classrooms are incentivised to back away from – when the goal is to gain marks in an objectively structured assessment, clarity is at a premium and nuance poorly rewarded. I don't have a solution to this issue in general, but when we have classes that are not leading to qualifications, where marks are not important, we should delight in difficult questions, in issues that don't admit a single answer – and on that note, which, no doubt, will have literature and politics teachers up in arms at my mathematician's simplicity, we will move onto the next challenge.

Chapter 9
A collection of miscellanea
(Or the joy of having choices)

Previous chapters may have led you to believe that the Cabinet of Curiosity is a carefully designed course where one session follows the next with a clockwork reliability that is understood by me, even if it masquerades as a surprise for the benefit of the students. You might also have come to expect a particular format of chapter in this book: the exposition of a topic followed by rumination on its value in developing curiosity with footnotes in the appendix for teachers who want to have a go themselves. As you by now hopefully recognise, I delight in complexity, nuance and intellectual mess and neither the Cabinet nor this book can be successfully constrained in this way forever. This is the chapter in which the wheels come off, either to careen into a canyon or to fly free into the skies. By way of a safety belt for this dangerous operation I can tell you that this chapter is a collection of topics, each of which has a session of its own when I deliver the course but which don't add enough individually to the idea of curiosity to deserve their own chapter in this book. Once we've rattled through dead languages, maps of the world, black holes, vitamin A, the Mountains of Kong and the history of India, there's a chapter on letting go of the lecture format completely – a departure from the structure of the Cabinet that paradoxically embraces the expression of curiosity. Buckle up, we're going for a ride.

The conceit of the Cabinet of Curiosity is that it contains an inexhaustible supply of curiosities from which we pluck something seemingly at random each week. The first time this course was run that was, indeed, a conceit – in fact, the sessions were numbered and very much limited to the number of lessons I had to fill. As time has gone by, however, I have added new sessions, put others into semi-retirement, and responded to requests from the class, ideas that have come up in discussion or simply the urges of my own idiosyncratic whim. There are now, therefore, far more than just eight sessions from which to draw upon, which makes things more interesting for me and enables me to be more responsive to the needs of the students.

One term, at the end of a session that, in retrospect, I can only imagine didn't tickle their fancy, a student asked if they were allowed to suggest topics for the Cabinet. I said they could suggest them but I was not making any promises and that, at any rate, it might take me a few weeks to put something coherent together. I can't remember how many suggestions the class made, but two of them survived to become lessons that worked well enough to have been used with other groups: the idea of dead languages and an introduction to the basic geography of the world.

Dead languages

We start by thinking about different language families, and particularly the Indo-European family which contains English and has the largest global reach (although not the greatest number of languages – it comes behind the Niger-Congo family that covers west and central Africa, the Austronesian family (Indonesia and Madagascar), Trans New Guinea (a large number of languages in a very small area of land) and Sino-Tibetan languages, which extend across China and down into southeast Asia).

The Indo-European family started in what is now Ukraine and spread outwards with migrating groups of people, splitting into different sub-families including Germanic (which includes English) and Balto-Slavic, which includes Livonian, the last European language to go extinct – which happened in 2013 when Grizelda Kristina died at the age of 103 in Canada. The story of the slow death of the Livonian language, and particularly the idea that the final native speaker was someone who had emigrated from the area as a child, is an interesting one that leads naturally into the question of language revival and protection (especially as Kristina's death sparked a movement to revive Livonian – a movement that currently has a couple of hundred members).

Welsh is an interesting case study here. The use of the language declined during the period of the Industrial Revolution but fears that it might die out were met by determined efforts during the twentieth century – particularly in requiring schools to teach it. I came across this in my first teaching job and saw that the flip side of protecting national identity and heritage was forcing a difficult and foreign language on young people who could see little purpose in it. The students in the Valleys comprehensive where I taught were proudly Welsh, but equally proudly English speaking – would their time have been better spent on something with more direct application?

There has been exactly one (large-scale) instance of a dead language being revived. Hebrew had survived as a language of ritual (in a similar way to Latin), but was nobody's native language until it was decided on as the national language of the nation of Israel. Since then, it has flourished and now has about five million native speakers, giving hope to Livonian, although in the ten years following Grizelda Kristina's death, a further 13 languages died out around the world – the direction of travel for linguistic diversity is almost entirely one-way.

Basic geography

Looking into different languages involves looking at maps of their distribution round the world and recognising that students don't always have a brilliant grasp of where things are. In response to this, the Cabinet contains a session on maps that starts with identifying places in the UK and reflecting on the advantages and limitations of my favoured sketch map of the British Isles:

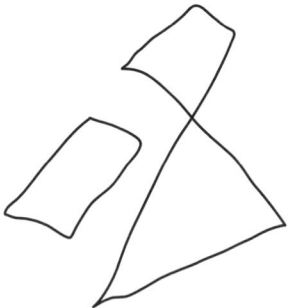

The British Isles (not drawn to scale)

We go on to look at Europe and the wider world before thinking about different projections and how they are created. The challenge for a cartographer is going from a curved globe to a flat sheet of paper while minimising distortion, and there is no perfect solution (other than sticking with the globe, although that has limitations as a book illustration).

Chapter 9 A collection of miscellanea

Two contrasting approaches illustrate this challenge (and provide some clarity on the use of the word 'projection' in relation to maps). In both, the idea is that we wrap a cylinder of paper round the globe to act as a screen, so that the cylinder touches the globe along the equator, and aim a light source at the surface of the sphere, projecting the image onto the cylindrical screen (which we can then uncurl and use as a flat map).

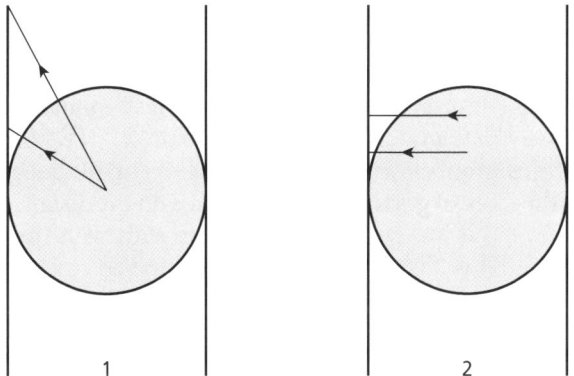

Projecting from the centre of the Earth (1) and projecting horizontally (2) to get different maps

In diagram 1, the light is a point at the centre of the globe and in diagram 2, there is a line of lights down the axis of the globe, all of which point horizontally. Both of these methods produce flat maps from the globe – the first one produces something like the Mercator projection and the second the Peters projection. You can see that in the first method, the distances between points (especially near the poles) are exaggerated compared with the second method. As a result of this, the area of, for example, Greenland looks much larger than it should in comparison with, for example, Africa. The second method preserves areas but makes the shapes look distorted as it reduces north/south distances (again, particularly near the poles).

This leads onto a discussion of other forms of projections including projecting onto a polyhedral surface rather than a cylinder, which makes a nice link to the many-sided dice of chapter 2. My favourite projection, however, is the Peirce Quincuncial which gets its name because it projects onto a square with the North Pole at the centre and the South Pole divided between the four corners (a quincunx is the distribution of five dots such as one might see on a die). The most charming thing about this is that the squares tessellate and could therefore be used to tile a floor – this is now one of my ambitions.

Black holes

A session on black holes was also a request from students and is another one that is a little heavy on the physics. For this reason I tend to choose between this one and quantum chromodynamics to run with a class. I prefer the charm of the octopus but black holes tend to be a bit more popular. We start with the basics: a black hole is a cosmic object with so much gravity that nothing – not even light – can move fast enough to escape from it. The key science to understand is escape velocity – if we fire a cannon into the sky, the cannonball will slow down due to gravity, but as it gets higher in the sky, the force of gravity (which depends on the distance from the Earth) decreases – if it was going fast enough to start with then it would never come back. This 'fast enough' is the escape velocity and doesn't depend on the mass of the cannonball. It does, however, depend on (and can be calculated from) the mass and radius of the Earth – it comes out as about 11 km s^{-1}, which is a lot faster than the speed of sound (0.3 km s^{-1}) and a lot slower than the speed of light (300,000 km s^{-1}).

Different planets, moons, stars and asteroids have their own escape velocities: for the Sun, it's about 618 km s^{-1} while for Deimos, the smaller of Mars' moons, it's just 5 m s^{-1}, which is not just slower than sound, but also slower than a decent running speed – if an Olympic high jumper were to enter a competition on Deimos, rather than clearing the bar and returning to the crash mat, their leap would continue upwards forever. None of these escape velocities is anywhere near the speed of light (which, remember, is what defines a black hole). To imagine a black hole we have to think of something much heavier or with a much smaller radius, or both. If, for example, you were to take the mass of the Sun and squeeze it into a ball a bit smaller than the Moon, you'd have an object that even light wasn't fast enough to escape – a black hole.

The theory is all very well (especially if you, as I just have, ignore anything that looks too difficult), but the practical question of whether an object like a black hole actually existed anywhere in the universe was an open one for a long time even after they had been imagined (and written about in science fiction). It's an interesting thought experiment to wonder how, armed with a telescope on Earth, one might go about searching the blackness of the night for a black hole – and once the challenge of that has sunk in we can tip our hats to Paul Murdin and Louise Webster who found Cygnus X-1 from the Australian desert back in 1971 and, with a diffident, 'It might be a black hole …', proved to the world that such things actually exist.

While some sessions have become fixtures of the Cabinet of Curiosity, favourites of mine and those that are likely to go down well with the students, others have withered away for one reason or another. That includes three from my original plan: a chemistry session on vitamin A, a history of India and some African geography based around the Mountains of Kong.

Vitamin A

Vitamin A is a really interesting compound that is required by the body for, among other things, providing light sensitivity in the eyes and is therefore responsible for the myth that carrots help you see in the dark (which they do, in that vitamin A deficiency can make night vision worse and carrots can bring you up to the baseline). In fact, vitamin A is a collection of compounds that have a similar structure and which the body can transform from one into another; these include retinol, retinal and beta-carotene.

Each of these compounds has two important structures: an ionone ring and an isoprene chain attached to it in the beta position. As these are unfamiliar to students and also, possibly, to you (and me), a diagram is appropriate:

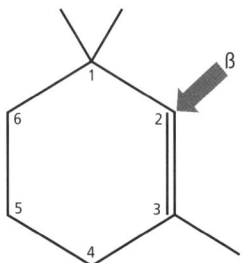

An ionone ring

The ionone ring is six carbons. In organic chemistry, the convention when drawing diagrams is that the carbon atoms mark the vertices of the shape and hydrogen atoms are left off to make the diagram clearer. This is not confusing or ambiguous because it's understood that each carbon makes four bonds (due to the immutable laws of electron shells) and so, if a carbon is shown as having fewer than four, we know to mentally add hydrogens back into the gaps. Two of these six carbons (2 and 3 in the diagram on the previous page) are joined with a double bond and two (1 and 3) have other carbons attached to them. The 'beta' carbon (2) is marked and has three of its four bonds already used, leaving just one to be attached to a hydrogen or, once we have it lined up, an isoprene chain.

```
H₃C              CH₂
   \            //
    C — C
   //       \
H₂C          H
```

An isoprene chain

Isoprene is a four-carbon chain with two double bonds and one extra carbon branching off. The carbons that have a double bond and two hydrogens (these are marked CH_2 in the diagram) can be used to attach this chain to other chains to make a longer molecule. In a minute we will see how two isoprenes and one ionone fit together with an alcohol group, CH_2OH, to make retinol but first, let's look at the importance of the double bonds with a simpler compound.

Double bonds in a carbon chain fix the shape of the molecule in one of two positions (molecules can spin around single bonds but not around double ones). We can see this with a simplified diagram that has just one double bond and carbons that are attached to a carbon chain on one side and a hydrogen on the other – the key point is that the chains can be on the same side of the carbons or on opposite sides and can't easily switch between the two. The two possibilities are called 'stereoisomers'. Isomers are different compounds made from the same atoms and 'stereo' means that the atoms are distinguished by their position in space rather than the order they are bonded in.

```
chain     chain        chain     hydrogen
    \    /                 \    /
     C═C         or         C═C
    /    \                 /    \
hydrogen hydrogen     hydrogen   chain
```

Two simple stereoisomers

It takes energy (which can be provided by certain wavelengths of light) to temporarily break the double bond in retinol and allow it to spin round. The movement means that the molecule has changed shape – a change that can be detected by the nerves of the eye, which can send a message to the brain. This message, telling us that light of a certain wavelength has reached a certain point on our retina, is our experience of sight.

Let us look at the whole retinol compound now. The bonds joining the pieces together are a lighter grey so you can see the separate components, but in reality they are indistinguishable from other carbon–carbon bonds:

Retinol

This is rather wonderful, but in abstraction it's rather short for a session and I've not found anywhere interesting for it to move onto. In practice, I've provided molecular modelling kits and got the class to build a retinol molecule (the 'ol' of retinol telling us to end the isoprene chain with an alcohol group – an oxygen atom attached to a hydrogen) and the reason that I don't use it much is that it's a bit of a palaver borrowing the kits from chemistry. A poor excuse perhaps.

The Mountains of Kong

The Mountains of Kong is another session that ended up being short of content. The story regards the Niger River, which has a rather confusing bend to it which led to it being discovered in two sections that were, for a couple of centuries, not joined together in the minds of the geographers. The source of the Niger is in the Guinea Highlands, not too far from the Sierra Leone coast, but instead of flowing west to the sea it flows northeastwards into the Mali desert, where the gradient drops sharply and it forms the Inner Niger Delta – a braided collection of streams that lose a huge amount of their flow to evaporation. The mouth of the Niger is where it flows almost due south into the Niger Delta (another one) on the Gulf of Guinea off the coast of Nigeria.

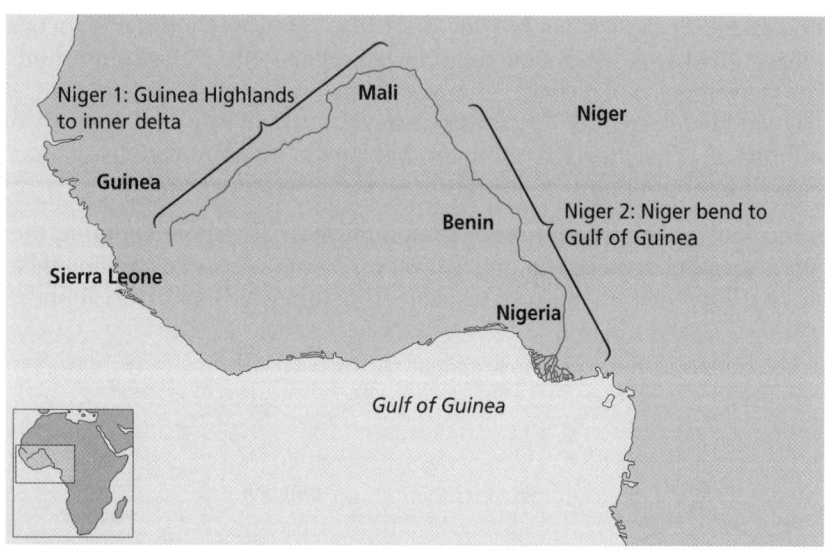

'Both' of these rivers were known to medieval Europeans who had trade with the kingdoms of both Mali, across the desert, and Benin, by ship along the coast. The river in the desert was known as the Niger (possibly from a Berber word) and the one flowing into the sea was called the Kworra (from a Hausa word).

The Mountains of Kong were one of the reasons that two and two were never put together – they were believed to form a huge range that runs parallel to the West African coast and then further east to become the source of the Nile. The cartographer James Rennell included them in a map of 1798 on the basis of the explorations of Mungo Park (an early explorer of the African interior) and, despite being entirely fictional, they continued to appear on maps throughout the nineteenth century. (According to Wikipedia, they even made it into an edition of Goode's atlas published in 1995. To be fair to Park, he was killed before he managed to achieve his goal of mapping the complete length of the upper river, which shows a laudable devotion to scholarship despite the diplomatic failings of his 'shoot first and pay no taxes' approach to local rulers. Goode also deserves better than to be remembered for this error so I will mention his homolosine projection – an equal-area projection that he developed to counter the distortions of the popular Mercator projection).

This is an excellent story which links to the session on maps and concludes with an object lesson in fact checking. Unfortunately, not only is it rather limited but I have concerns about telling an African story from the perspective of the Europeans – even when it turns out the Europeans were wrong. I have tried to adapt the session to include more of the people and cultures that live along the course of the Niger, but I don't have the depth of historical and geographical knowledge to be confident that I'm doing it sensitively. I have, instead, a session on the political geography of Africa which simply goes through all 54 countries in order of land area.

The history of India

The session on Indian history comes at the opposite end of the content range – there being far too much to fit into 40 minutes – but also has sensitivity issues with the challenge of giving the British Empire an appropriate weight among all the other empires that have, at some stage in the last 4000 years, ruled some or most of the subcontinent and, particularly, in giving a fair exposition on the events of 1857 (known to the British of the time as the Indian Mutiny but perhaps more fairly described as the First War of Independence).

I've tried a couple of approaches to condensing this huge history into something accessible – looking at India's empires chronologically either by land area or using a timeline similar to the one I used with the Stone Age. In either case, we start with the Indus Valley civilisation which occupied northwestern India from pre-history to about 1300 BC. It was replaced by the Vedic culture which brought with it the Indo-European language family (it is thought that the Indus Valley civilisation used Dravidic languages – a family that has since been pushed to the south of India and into Sri Lanka) and a form of literature including the Vedas from which it takes its name and which are the oldest texts of Hinduism.

Neither of these civilisations was an empire but rather a collection of cities and kingdoms, one of the most important of which was Magadha on the Ganges, that became the power base of the Mauryan Empire which was the largest by land area ever to occupy India. Magadha was also the birthplace of Buddhism, although parts of the empire favoured Jainism. The Mauryan Empire reached its peak under Ashoka (the Great) in the third century BC. Ashoka is a well-attested historical character and/but most of the information we have on him comes from Buddhist legends that present him as an idealisation of an emperor.

Following the Mauryan Empire was Classical India, 200 BC–AD 1200 – a succession of kingdoms and empires, the largest of which was the Gupta (around AD 375), which peaked as the fourth largest of India's empires. The Guptas were predominantly Hindu, but the next large empire – the Delhi Sultanate, reaching its maximal extent in the 1300s as the sixth largest – had Muslim rulers. The Delhi Sultanate was overthrown by the Mughals, led by Babur, a chieftain from Uzbekistan. The Mughals were responsible for the Taj Mahal and the influence of Persian on Old Hindi which led to modern Hindi and Urdu, and at their peak (in about 1700) had an even larger empire than the Guptas (this puts them third on the list, if you're keeping track).

During the 1700s, the Maratha Confederacy took over an increasingly large portion of central India but were, meanwhile, engaged in a series of wars with the British who, over a century and a half, built up an increasing hold on India via either direct rule or control over client kingdoms and principalities. The British, in this case, were not the British government but the East India Company which had originally been given a trading monopoly but had built up both its army (made up predominantly of sepoys – Indian soldiers under British officers) and political control.

One of the key ways in which the British gained territories was through the 'doctrine of lapse', which said that if an Indian prince died without a direct male heir, his lands would be handed over to British rule. This caused disquiet among the Indian ruling classes and contributed to the events of 1857 in which the soldiers working for the British revolted, at least partly due to the introduction of Christianity and the disregard for the Muslim and Hindu religions. It was a war with considerable atrocity on both sides and requires more time, space and scholarship than I am able to give it to do it justice. The conclusion was a British victory and the replacement of East Indian Company rule with the direct authority of the British crown. The British Empire – or Raj – lasted from 1857 to 1947 and was only beaten for size among Indian empires by the Maurya many centuries before.

After the Second World War, the Raj was partitioned into a Hindu state – modern India – and a Muslim one – Pakistan, from which Bangladesh split in 1971. Partition took place in August 1947 and left millions on the 'wrong' side of the line: Hindus in the new state of Pakistan and Muslims in independent India. The upheaval led to violence, hundreds of thousands of deaths and a soured international relationship that lasts to this day. The creation of Bangladesh was, if anything, less peaceful, following a civil war that lasted the best part of 1971 and led to between 300,000 and 3 million civilian deaths. Modern India is a democratic, federal, multi-lingual, pluralistic society which is the seventh largest country by land area and largest by population in the world. It is also, according to the preamble to its constitution, a secular state, in which 80% are Hindu, 14% Muslim, 2% Christian, 2% Sikh (Sikhism as a religion began in northwest India during the Delhi Sultanate) and 1% Buddhist. (Having been the dominant religion under the Mauryan Empire and maintaining influence under the Guptas, Buddhism declined quickly and was almost eliminated from India by the 1200s.)

The history of India might not appear very often in the course, but in some ways it encapsulates the ethos of the Cabinet of Curiosity better than other sessions – there is so much to say and so many different ways of telling the story. (I suspect that if it has another incarnation, then it will be through the lens of religion with Hinduism, Buddhism, Islam, Sikhism and Christianity all playing their part.) The session raises more questions than it satisfactorily answers and to most of them the only response I have is, 'I don't know, let's find out for next week.' I wonder if it could be a rich resource that I dip into when relevant, inspired by world events, but until then the slides, a bit jumbled and desultory, sit in the collection awaiting their moment.

Rationale and reflections

Curiosity is a superpower – if you have got this far without agreeing with me on this then I salute your independence of thought. Part of the superness of that power is that it is unending – with curiosity in your back pocket you need never be bored. It is therefore always going to be the case that my lesson slides get added to and reorganised as my own curiosity brings me to new understandings both of teaching students and of the broad sweep of academic study (which includes, but is not limited to, the entirety of astronomy, biology, history and geography, which was what Pippin demanded of Gandalf as they rode towards Minas Tirith. I guess I'm just a more demanding student than your average hobbit).

Teaching curiosity requires subjects that are interesting and accessible to the audience, that excite and charm the teacher (I cannot over-emphasise the value of enthusiasm), that reach a satisfying conclusion while throwing out bigger questions, and that fit together into an interconnected whole that covers a fair swathe of disciplines. There can therefore be no perfect mix and certainly no recipe that one person could pass on to another (and I'm sorry if that was what you were hoping for when you read the introduction). Every class is different in composition and experience and exists in a different environment of current affairs (of all the things we hope to make students curious about, surely the state of the world in which they actually live is close to the top of the list).

As well as all of those purposes, the Cabinet of Curiosity sessions are designed to create a classroom community with a questioning ethos – an environment in which ideas are welcomed, challenged and chewed over rather than dismissed; where dissenting arguments are relished and treasured; where being wrong is the door to finding out rather than a shame to be avoided. The culmination of this spirit comes in enabling students to choose the topic for discussion and to provide the content in terms of their own knowledge, experience and opinions. In my view, the real success of someone who owns a cabinet of curiosity comes not in showing off its delights to adoring visitors but in the moment when those visitors start putting their own cabinets together – cabinets that are not merely reflections of the original but that build on it, rejecting some parts and adding new content. This wasn't a universal belief among the Renaissance scholars who compiled the first cabinets of curiosity; there was definitely some one-upmanship, but I'm convinced that mine is the right approach from a twenty-first century educational perspective. Our final chapter takes this idea further and explores the idea of communal, co-created, discursive, democratic curiosity.

Chapter 10
Throwing open to the floor (Or how I stopped worrying and learned to love the unknown)

The Cabinet of Curiosity was conceived as an endless succession of ideas that I would bring to the group and expound upon – and there are, as explored in previous chapters, more sessions than can be accommodated in an eight-week course. However, not only do I now have a choice of which sessions to lay before a particular group of students, I have added a new ingredient – the unpredictable unknown. It seemed to me desirable that I should not be the only one bringing ideas to the room; that a series of lectures, excellent in its own way, was limited in the demands it placed on the students. I now try to construct sessions in which students share their thoughts, fascinations and views with each other. At their best, these sessions are freewheeling, fast-paced conversations which flit from the serious (knife crime) to the light-hearted (comparative merits of netball and soccer); from the sublime (the meaning of beauty) to the ridiculous (any one of a number of conspiracy theories I've had to try to quash). As you might imagine, getting to the freewheeling is the hard part: as with cycling, there is usually a hill to climb first.

With any new group I always start with a few standard sessions – taken from the menu of my rolling slide deck or, occasionally, inspired by a request from a student. This allows me to set out my expectations of listening, paying attention, participating when called upon and being ready to take notes should I say something interesting (a phenomenon that some students observe more frequently than others). I am also able to take stock of the individuals, work out who will be most willing to offer ideas and whose ideas will be most worthy of the class attention (they are not always the same person). I also use this time to get them used to setting the room up in a horseshoe shape, which is extremely useful for class discussions as they can all see each other's faces – it's unfortunately not very space efficient but so far I've managed to avoid having either a room too small or a group too big.

The challenge is in getting started, equipping enough students with the curiosity to wonder about the world, the confidence to share that wondering with others and the skill to say something interesting. Given how much energy I put into having something interesting to say, it seems appropriate to ask them to do some homework and come prepared to the session with ideas of their own. One way of doing this has been to ask them all to think of something they think is interesting, something to debate and something they would like to know more about and to put all the class suggestions onto a page to share with them. This encourages them to think about something, to have prepared an idea of where they would like the conversation to go. It also provides a question that can't be ducked out of – while it is easy for a student to say, 'I don't know' when you ask what we should talk about, it's not so reasonable if you ask them to pick a topic from the list they've all contributed to.

There are lots of reasons why students might be unwilling to talk in the unstructured environment I'm aiming to create, but enabling and encouraging them to do so is a key goal. One of the joys of curiosity is sharing it with others, and one of the key sources of interest is conversations with those whose curiosities overlap but are not the same as one's own. The most common reason for reluctance to speak is being unsure of the expectations: not knowing what one is allowed to say, what response one can expect, and not wanting to get into trouble or cause upset. Creating a framework for engagement – via a list of topics – is one way of overcoming this, but it is also important to moderate the responses of the group. For the discussion to work, students need to be confident that they won't have their ideas laughed at, dismissed or shouted down and so it's important as the teacher to find something interesting and sensible in every contribution and to support, both by encouragement and airtime, minority views. As a student, finding that what you are saying has most of the class nodding in agreement doesn't make you right and may well make you less interesting (if only that everyone has heard that particular argument already).

Another reason to be quiet is feeling that you don't know enough or not being sure enough of your thoughts or opinions to say anything meaningful. This is another area where preparation makes a big difference: you might not be able to say anything sensible about someone else's topic, but you should be able to have a thought on your own. Because of this, I often go to the least-confident students to start a session (although not the first one in this format – being the first of the first requires substantial self-confidence) and usually have the rule that anyone called upon to speak can respond to what has already been said or, if they feel it has been played out, can start us on a new topic. Sometimes this can lead to a rather bewildering conversation in which two (or even three) topics are going on at once, with students choosing which strand they wish to pitch in on. I quite enjoy this kind of chaos but have drawn the line at introducing a fourth topic: that would just be silly.

Laziness can be a driver in some students, although I'm careful not to overdiagnose this: listening and thinking and formulating thoughts all take effort and students can be used to getting away with passivity in classes. They can also come to the Cabinet deeming it irrelevant to their ambitions, not a proper lesson, or even a waste of time (my anguish at this suggestion is something I like to ham up). I have also had students whose sleep regime does not follow my wise and oft-repeated precepts (no daytime naps, devices off at 9pm, in bed by 10pm, alarm set for 6am and the snooze button is your enemy) and who are minded to catch up during the lesson. Light mockery of those peacefully dozing is, I think, completely justified once I'm confident that there are no pastoral issues that need following up more seriously.

Another opportunity to provide students with the preparation needed comes if I've had to be absent for a session. There is no textbook for the Cabinet (at least not before this book was published) and so working out how to enable students to use the time effectively without my presence has been a bit of a challenge. I have worked on two stock 'cover' lessons, both of which provide students with some reading to do, to be followed by a piece of writing. The first is the story of the Jallianwala Bagh Massacre (also known as the Massacre of Amritsar), one of the shadiest episodes of the British Raj period of Indian history. I provide them with the following material adapted from a Wikipedia entry on the subject (see https://en.wikipedia.org/wiki/Jallianwala_Bagh_massacre).

During World War I, British India contributed to the British war effort by providing men and resources. Millions of Indian soldiers and labourers served in Europe, Africa, and the Middle East, while both the Indian administration and the princes sent large supplies of food, money, and ammunition. Bengal [North East India] and Punjab [North West India] remained sources of anti-colonial activities. Revolutionary attacks in Bengal, associated increasingly with disturbances in Punjab, were enough to nearly paralyse the regional administration. Of these, a pan-Indian mutiny in the British Indian Army planned for February 1915 was the most prominent amongst a number of plots formulated between 1914 and 1917 by Indian nationalists in India, the United States and Germany.

The planned February mutiny was ultimately thwarted. Mutinies in smaller units and garrisons within India were also crushed. In the context of the British war effort and the threat from the separatist movement in India, the Defence of India Act 1915 was passed, limiting civil and political liberties. Michael O'Dwyer, then the Lieutenant Governor of Punjab, was one of the strongest proponents of the act.

The passage of the Rowlatt Act [which continued emergency legislation that let, for example, police arrest any person without reason] in 1919 precipitated large-scale political unrest throughout India. Ominously, in 1919, the Third Anglo-Afghan War began in the wake of Amir Habibullah's assassination [Afghanistan borders Punjab]. Muhammad Ali Jinnah [a politician and barrister] resigned from his Bombay seat, writing in a letter to the Viceroy, 'I, therefore, as a protest against the passing of the Bill and the manner in which it was passed tender my resignation ... a Government that passes or sanctions such a law in times of peace forfeits its claim to be called a civilised government.' [Mahatma] Gandhi's call for protest against the Rowlatt Act achieved an unprecedented response of furious unrest and protests.

Especially in Punjab, the situation was deteriorating rapidly, with disruptions of rail, telegraph and communication systems. The movement was at its peak before the end of the first week of April, with some recording that 'practically the whole of Lahore was on the streets, the immense crowd that passed through Anarkali Bazaar was estimated to be around 20,000'. Many officers in the Indian army believed revolt was possible, and they prepared for the worst. Michael O'Dwyer is said to have believed that these were the early and ill-concealed signs of a conspiracy for a coordinated revolt planned around May.

On 11 April, Marcella Sherwood, an elderly English missionary, fearing for the safety of the approximately 600 Indian children under her care, was on her way to shut the schools and send the children home. While travelling through a narrow street called the Kucha Kurrichhan, she was caught by a mob who violently attacked her. She was rescued by some local Indians, including the father of one of her pupils, who hid her from the mob and then smuggled her to safety. After visiting Sherwood on 19 April, the local commander of Indian Army forces, Brigadier General Dyer, enraged at the assault, issued an order requiring every Indian man using that street to crawl its length on his hands and knees as a punishment. Dyer later explained to a British inspector: 'Some Indians crawl face downwards in front of their gods. I wanted them to know that a British woman is as sacred as a Hindu god and therefore they have to crawl in front of her, too.' He also authorised the indiscriminate public whipping of locals who came within lathi length [a baton about three feet long] of a police officer.

On Sunday, 13 April 1919, Dyer, convinced that a major insurrection could take place, banned all meetings. This notice was not widely disseminated, and thousands of villagers gathered in the Jallianwala Bagh [a park in Amritsar, Punjab] to celebrate the Baisakhi festival and peacefully protest against the arrest and deportation of two national leaders.

Many who were present had been worshipping earlier at the Golden Temple and were merely passing through the Bagh on their way home. The Bagh was (and remains today) an open area of six to seven acres, roughly 200 yards by 200 yards in size, and surrounded on all sides by walls roughly 10 feet in height. Balconies of houses three to four stories tall overlooked the Bagh, and five narrow entrances opened onto it, several with lockable gates. Although it was planted with crops during the rainy season, for much of the rest of the year it served as a local meeting place and recreation area.

An hour after the meeting began as scheduled at 17:30, Colonel Dyer arrived at the Bagh with a group of 50 troops. All fifty were armed with .303 Lee–Enfield bolt-action rifles. Dyer may have specifically chosen troops from ethnic groups due to their proven loyalty to the British. He had also brought two armoured cars armed with machine guns; however, the vehicles could not enter the compound through the narrow entrances. The main entrance was relatively wide, but was guarded heavily by the troops backed by the armoured vehicles so as to prevent anyone from getting out.

Without warning the crowd to disperse, Dyer ordered his troops to block the main exits and begin shooting toward the densest sections of the crowd in front of the available narrow exits, where panicked crowds were trying to leave the Bagh. Firing continued for approximately ten minutes. Unarmed civilians, including men, women, elderly people and children were killed. This incident came to be known as the Amritsar massacre. A cease-fire was ordered after the troops fired about one third of their ammunition. He stated later that the purpose of this action 'was not to disperse the meeting but to punish the Indians for disobedience'.

The following day Dyer stated in a report, 'I have heard that between 200 and 300 of the crowd were killed. My party fired 1650 rounds.' Apart from the many deaths that resulted directly from the shooting, a number of people died by being crushed in the stampedes at the narrow gates or by jumping into the solitary well on the compound to escape the shooting. Dyer imposed a curfew time that was earlier than the usual time; as a result, the wounded could not be moved from where they had fallen, and many of them therefore died of their wounds during the night.

Colonel Dyer reported to his superiors that he had been 'confronted by a revolutionary army'. Both Secretary of State for War Winston Churchill and former Prime Minister H.H. Asquith, however, openly condemned the attack, Churchill referring to it as 'unutterably monstrous', and Asquith calling it 'one of the worst, most dreadful, outrages in the whole of our history'. MPs voted 247 to 37 against Dyer and in support of the Government. Despite the official rebuke, many Britons still 'thought him a hero for saving the rule of British law in India'. This event caused many moderate Indians to abandon their previous loyalty to the British and become nationalists distrustful of British rule. Rabindranath Tagore [an Indian poet] renounced his knighthood as a symbolic act of protest, saying 'I wish to stand, shorn of all special distinctions, by the side of those of my countrymen who, for their so-called insignificance, are liable to suffer degradation not fit for human beings.'

I ask the students to write notes on this and then reflect on the idea that very few people are mad or evil: most of the awful episodes of human history are due to ordinary people behaving badly because they are frightened or angry. This provides a useful starting point for discussion in the following session – was Dyer ordinary and frightened, or mad or evil? In general, they tend to be very willing to condemn Dyer rather than recognise the failings of the human condition, but then there are others in the story whose behaviour falls short of the high standards to which we would hold ourselves (I say, theatrically).

Another cover session is based around another Yeats poem: *Sailing to Byzantium*. I provide students with an annotated copy of the text with words explained, allusions developed and some of my own personal reflections. I then ask them to focus in on the language of the poem via four questions.

1. Look at the whole poem. What actions, feelings and thoughts is the poet describing? How do these shift?
2. Pick a stanza of your choice. Describe what is literally said and analyse the imagery of the stanza.
3. Choose a couplet (two adjacent lines) that appeals to you. Explain why you chose this and why it is interesting.
4. Select one word that hits hard in this poem. Evaluate the poet's choice of this word.

Students find this poem very hard – I wouldn't feel confident putting it to a group that I hadn't spent a few weeks warming up (the Jallianwala Bagh piece is more accessible). Looking at language and how it is used is, however, something that I think is important – clear and beautiful communication is a huge employability skill that can be almost indefinitely developed – and the structure here usually allows them to say something intelligent. It also means that we are able to spend the next session discussing Yeats' thesis that we are all so caught up in what he describes euphemistically as 'sensual music' that we neglect the monuments of 'unageing intellect' that are available to those who focus on study.

Whatever the topic of discussion, managing it requires a lot of concentration in order to ensure that thoughts that need challenging are challenged, that students who have something to say but won't volunteer are called upon, that students who have too much to say are given their time in the limelight but reined in when necessary, that topics that make people uncomfortable are handled sensitively (or in some cases cut short), and that I find a way of enticing everyone to say something. I sit at the front facing the class with a desk in front of me so that I can take notes (of who has spoken or of interesting points I want to come back to) and interject when I think I can be helpful (actually one of my biggest challenges is making sure that their voices are heard more than mine, of which I'm inordinately fond.)

A final form of this session comes where I have a theme for us to work around and one of my favourites is to ask them for the most beautiful thing in the world. This might be a painting (we have had Van Gogh's *The Starry Night*) or a photograph (the 1984 photograph of Sharbat Gula entitled 'Afghan Girl' was suggested one year), a piece of music (Dire Straits' *Telegraph Road* was introduced to me this way) or an abstract idea (and we have been set off on a discussion of kindness as a result). The power of the internet and a projector allows me to share the suggestions and get feedback, and it is a sign that the group is going well when students are willing to articulate what they find beautiful.

I have also asked for stories: fairy stories, folk stories, true stories, family adventures. This has not gone so smoothly – stories can be hard to tell and students are not confident of their narrative ability – but has always been interesting. One thing that makes it go better is when I have a story or two up my sleeve to indicate the kind of thing I'm hoping for – that choice definitely guides the subsequent suggestions and there is no point expecting them to follow a fairy story with a tale of their childhood (or vice versa). This is usually a session I save for the end of the course, partly because I feel it is an indulgence, given that some of the class will get away without contributing much, and partly because I think they need to be really confident in each other in order to give it a go. Indulgent, maybe, but gloriously curious as we share the stories that make us who we are, that lie at the heart of our cultures. One of the challenges laid down in chapter 1 was the question of who decides which stories count as 'cultural capital' and our answer here in chapter 10 is that we do.

Confidence is at the heart of this version of the Cabinet and the first time I tried it I was very nervous of the unknown, of the idea that we could end up talking about anything or simply be faced with an embarrassment of silent pauses. In some ways it's the antithesis of the tightly controlled mini-lectures that have gone before. I wasn't sure that they would have anything to say, and I was concerned that what they wanted to talk about would be unhelpful or that I wouldn't know enough to provide accuracy and keep us on the straight and narrow. One conversation, in which one student wished to talk admiringly about Andrew Tate, was definitely in this area and I was concerned that given free rein, students might say things that made themselves look foolish or that were hurtful to others. Ensuring ideas are challenged without giving airtime to views that would be best left unexpressed is occasionally a tricky line to walk. Happily, my worries have been, by and large, unfounded and these sessions are the ones the students value most highly – the privilege of being able to share their own views and hear those of their peers is one they have appreciated. At the end of the course I ask for a reflection and I receive a cheering quantity of affirmation from the joyful enthusiasts, but it is also common for a few students to say something along the lines of, 'I know I didn't say much in the debates, but I really enjoyed them and will try to do better next time I'm in this situation.' Curiosity is a spectrum and at the incurious end there is a region of infrared. Those who have made the decision to step into visible curiosity might not end up as brightly violet as I'd like but have still moved in the right direction so I take that as a win.

Chapter 11
The curiosity toolkit
(Or what I've learned from 20 cohorts and two schools)

Part of a good toolkit is the toolbox it sits in, part of it is an impressive collection of spanners, but the most important aspect is knowing which tools need to be in it and how to pick the right one for each job.

Since I came up with the idea of the Cabinet of Curiosity, I've run it with four quite different approaches to selecting students for the class and each of these has provided different demands and has taught me something new about curiosity and the teaching thereof. If chapter 10 was the moment when content and rationale became inextricably entwined, then this is where the practicalities that have hitherto been consigned to the appendix come into view. This chapter looks at different manifestations of curiosity in my experience of teaching it – I hope that my experience will be useful to anyone tempted to have a go at making their own cabinet while remaining interesting to those who are here for the narrative.

The original conception at Harris Westminster was to pick out students who were noted for their lack of curiosity and for the sessions to do some heavy lifting in encouraging them to engage more fervently with the marvels of learning. The school is highly selective, with students passing through an entrance exam and interview before getting an offer conditional on GCSE results; this structure is designed to pick out those with potential rather than relying entirely on attainment as measured by grades. As a result, the majority of students are not just bright, but interesting, motivated and enthusiastic about the prospect of learning.

The system is, however, also designed to collect those who could be these things with the right nurturing but whose thirst for knowledge is hidden beneath sediments of boredom and anxiety, whose schooling thus far has encouraged them to keep their heads down, conceal their brilliance and get away with as little effort as possible. For such students, the Cabinet of Curiosity was created and it has served them well, despite some heroic battles over the minimal acceptable level of engagement.

At the end of the course, I ask students to produce a reflection on their time in the Cabinet. They have two sessions to work on it and are expected to do any further finishing off in their own time; my expectation is that it will take them something like a further 40 minutes if they exert themselves adequately in class time. I am prepared to receive this reflection (or 'response' in the HWSF vernacular) in any format, but when it seems that some direction would be helpful, I suggest that they might like to fill a page of A4 with facts presented as interestingly and attractively as possible and append to this, using a fastening of their choice, exactly 143 words of personal reflection on the experience of the course. I usually get asked, 'Why exactly 143 words?' – not to do so would represent a considerable lack of curiosity – and there are a couple of reasons, as well as the assessment value of provoking that question. The first thing is that I want neither an eight-page essay nor a six-word grunt, and a word count gives an indication of how much I want. The second is that I want them to think about their words, to tailor their effort to the restrictions and to use a bit of imagination when putting it together. As an alternative, I ask for a couple of pages about something that they find interesting and hope that I might too. This second version has drawn some students into temptation, labouring as they were under the misapprehension that I, like the teacher in *What Katy Did at School*, would not read essays they submit – or else that I'm too stupid to recognise content scraped from the internet. Plagiarism scores badly, as you might expect, but also incurs penance in the form of a longer essay to be written by hand.

What has interested me is that fairly often, when I have managed to squeeze an adequate word count from my recalcitrant prey, their final 143 words have reflected on the experience and that they would have got more out of it had they been more willing from the beginning. This reaffirms my view that more teenagers than is generally appreciated are splendid – some just don't know it yet. It also confirms my belief that curiosity is a universal human trait, that it's something that everyone can enjoy as well as benefit from, that it's not some strange luxury or esoteric delight of the academically able, but an activity that's available to all in return for a modicum of effort. Not so secretly, I suspect that a large part of the difference between the academically successful and those who are less so is the unrestrained indulgence in curiosity.

The second type of group at Harris Westminster has been formed when the course has been offered as an option together with all the other Cultural Perspective titles. I don't know exactly what causes someone to choose the Cabinet of Curiosity rather than 'Origami for Beginners', 'Synthesis of Aspirin' or 'The History of Feminism', but I guess it is some combination of being amused by my particular brand of whimsy, wanting to get to know the Principal better, misclicking the choices menu, and genuine curiosity. This kind of group has brought students who have been enthusiastic to share their insights and we have often quickly moved to the discussion sessions – more than ever, the skill has been to keep some of the comments short and to the point. In one of these groups, one of the students offered feedback on each of the sessions, identifying things that went well and potential improvements (which was welcome, if not always comfortable), and in another, the students demanded that I organise a trip to the National Gallery one lunchtime so that we could see the art that I'd told them about.

One thing that is interesting is that no two groups are the same, despite having the same kind of make-up, and so no two editions of the Cabinet of Curiosity are the same. I suppose this is true of all teaching, and is why we never get bored, but I've particularly noticed it here – partly, I guess, because of the freedom to follow a trail, to pick up on the interests of the students and allow them to direct our destination without worrying about hitting all the syllabus content or understanding the mark scheme.

We've used a similar method at Harris Clapham Sixth Form and found some differences in the cohorts: here the students are more socially conservative and less used to exploring and articulating their own views. There has therefore been some real joy in opening ideas and watching them listen to each other. They are less prone to challenging what others say and more likely to simply agree with the last person when put on the spot, which has put greater weight on the written work produced – without a watching audience they are able to be more reflective and incisive.

Finally, also at Harris Clapham, we've used the Cabinet as part of our 'Competitive Universities Pathway', with the idea being that in order to get into the top destinations, students need to supplement the content of their classes with reading and thinking of their own – and that in order to take the step into doing this, they need to have their curiosity piqued. Since this has turned the Cabinet into a one-year course, tripling its length, I've had to add some additional sessions, bringing in some logic problems as well as a brief history of Ukraine. The logic session was, as one might expect, highly interactive and students enjoyed thinking through the challenges which were similar to this one:

You meet three people, Petunia, Samad and Roshaun.

- One tells the truth if nobody has spoken before them and otherwise lies.
- One tells the truth if nobody has spoken before them or if the previous person lied and otherwise lies.
- One sometimes tells the truth and sometimes lies completely unpredictably.

They make the following statements:

Petunia: 'Exactly three of these statements are true.'

Samad: 'Exactly two of these statements are true.'

Roshaun: 'Exactly one of these statements is true.'

Samad: 'None of these statements is true.'

The students have to work out:

- Which, if any, of these statements is true?
- Who tells the truth completely unpredictably?

This kind of puzzle is appropriate for a 'toolbox' chapter because cracking it open requires finding the right way of looking at it. The general approach is to make conjectures and, assuming you guessed wrong, to use the insights that being wrong gives you to move towards being right.

In this case, one might suppose Petunia was telling the truth and calculate what that would mean. Three people telling the truth is impossible since the statements are mutually exclusive, so in this case we immediately work out that no more than one statement can be true. With this insight, it is a task left to the reader (that's you) to work out exactly what is true and, from that, which of the three people fits each of the descriptions.

The next logic problem would require a different spanner to loosen its grip, but for each one the approach of supposing something and seeing where that supposition gets you is a useful starting point. It's an approach that translates well – while there are some problems that you need to be confident of before having a go, with most things you get further by diving in than staring blankly at the empty page. Thomas Edison didn't quite say, 'I have not failed, I now know 3000 ways not to make a lightbulb', but that's only because he needed better editing – his method was exactly this one of learning through trial and failure.

We are still only halfway through this incarnation of the course and so I will need to come up with some more sessions – although, there is, of course, an almost inexhaustible supply of free-flowing conversation, the only limit being the imagination and curiosity of the group. My plan is to do some work with them on personal statements – not from the point of view of crafting the perfect combination of earnest devotion to their chosen subject and demonstration of their collection of appropriate skills; but with a view to helping them to find out what interests them and what it is about them that might interest a university or employer. I think this is both the largest benefit of the personal statement (which is surely almost useless to universities), but also its greatest limitation: students who embrace the process wholeheartedly will, by writing a personal statement, put themselves in a better position to make a success of an undergraduate course, but students who don't already have a degree of curiosity find themselves in difficulty when they have a box not just to tick but to fill with intelligent sentences.

No matter what is finally written, the actual process of writing a personal statement (I will be teaching my class) begins with thinking about what you want to study and why you want to study it: what you are interested in, what you would like to learn more about, what it is that fires your curiosity. There is then a reflection on what skills are required to do well – mostly these are academic competences but such things as capacity for hard work and good organisation and timekeeping are also valuable. Armed with a kind of list, students will need to think about how their experiences so far (and particularly their recent experiences, in the sixth form or Year 11) have helped them to develop their skills. I hope that going through this process will inspire them to be more interested and interesting and to use some of their Year 12 summer to address any gaps that they find.

I'm also reflecting on the gaps in the Cabinet of Curiosity; what sessions could we add, what aspects of the world do I say little about, what would I like to learn more about? Geographically, we have little from East Asia or South America; historically, a gaping void between the Old Stone Age and the eighteenth century; scientifically, there's more physics than chemistry or biology; artistically, nothing on music. From a literary point of view, as well as the poems of Yeats (and there are always more poets to include), I have a session on what makes writing beautiful with excerpts from James Joyce's *Dubliners,* Julian Barnes' *A History of the World in 10½ Chapters,* Joseph Conrad's *Youth,* Antoine de Saint-Exupéry's *The Little Prince* and Gabriel García Márquez's *Love in the Time of Cholera.* I've nothing on Classics and there's a rich vein of Greek myth to be mined (far too rich for a single session unless I find an interesting way of cutting it down). I think that if I decided I needed another mathematics session (I'm not at all sure I do, but it's always a temptation) then it would be Euclidean geometry. (I very much enjoy teaching Group Theory, but that takes eight weeks all on its own.) I think that economics, religion and philosophy are best approached through the conversation sessions, exploring students' thoughts on questions that come up. I'm happy with the politics content (at least until someone suggests that I look into Brazil's democratic system) and I'm not sure that a single session on any particular language would be enough to drive meaningful curiosity.

I claimed this chapter was a toolkit – in fact, I think the whole book is a toolkit, but only if you think of the contents as prepared cores, those riverbed rocks roughly chipped to shape. Maybe the book so far has been an attempt to describe those prepared cores, to give an indication of the purposes to which each might be turned – I certainly hope it's been something more than a pretty box in which I've stored my collection of old rocks.

The point of this chapter is to turn rocks into hammers, knives, drill bits, screwdrivers and trusty Allen keys. Each cohort of students needs a different presentation; each session can be adapted to the context in which it's delivered. Different subjects align themselves naturally with different purposes and choosing the right approach is a skill in itself. Here are some of the ways I think that different sessions have enabled my cabinet to work.

- Drawing networks takes students into a weird world where asking questions feels normal and there being interesting answers is a joyous surprise. It also gives me the confidence to focus on getting to know the students without worrying about remembering the content.
- Rattling through the Palaeolithic gives students a sense of how much there is that they just don't know while tying together what they've learned in history and biology and raising big questions of religion and race.

- The politics of my youth opens the lid on a period that lies just beyond their personal experience, provides some background on current affairs and gives them permission to be interested in the news.
- Turner and Constable invite them into high culture and show how accessible it can be, even through the eyes of a mathematically minded beginner.
- The rough beast, slouching towards Bethlehem, is a piece of verbal theatre where words dance and delight. It exemplifies the art of allusion, of being able to mean more than you say because both sides of the conversation have a shared pool of knowledge. It epitomises the value of cultural capital.
- The subatomic octopus shows how even the wrongest of answers can lead to interesting questions, that subjects far from your heart can be interesting and that you don't need to understand all the detail to be fascinated by it.
- American politics proposes the idea that the devil is in the detail, that there is more going on than there appears and that systems work, when they do, because people have thought really hard about ensuring that they do.

There are some sharp edges, but the most important tool of all is the hammer. 'Learning is amazing,' I say, and I continue to say it whatever eye rolls, groans or looks of dull indifference come my way. I hammer away at this idea, reclothing it with new content, repackaging it with new questions, and I continue to hammer away until the students recognise that this is no façade. The stereotype of teenaged response that I offered at the start of this paragraph is an affectation, a world-weary cynicism from young people who think they're being tricked into learning. The cynicism is a carapace designed to protect them from the adult world, and it wouldn't be a stereotype if it were easy to remove, but bloody-minded perseverance (and a trusty hammer) is more effective in my experience of teaching than it ever has been in DIY. Eventually it dawns on the students that I believe what I say, that I delight in the ideas I'm sharing with them, that the process of finding out, of learning, is one I revel in.

My final challenge is to you, the reader – where has this book left you? I hope that you have found some of the subjects interesting and that you have both learned something and been sparked into additional curiosity to check my assertions (I've done my best, but please send me corrections and I'll do my best with a second edition) or to enquire more deeply.

If you're a teacher, then I hope I've set you wondering whether you could put together a similar course for your students in your setting – and if not (because of timetables or structures or the simple challenge of fitting into what there already is), I hope you're wondering whether there is some other way in which you can encourage curiosity in your students.

If you're a school leader, then I hope you're encouraged by the possibilities of this course and are thinking about how it might work in your school – I hope you are hoping that one of your teachers has also read the book and will knock on your door to ask whether they can run the course (idea: buy them a copy!).

If you're a parent, grandparent, godparent, uncle, aunt or simply someone who has dealings with the younger generation, then I hope you have picked up some conversation starters that might inspire some curiosity.

And if you're a teenager, then I really hope you have enjoyed the book and that you have been convinced by my central thesis – *curiosity is a superpower* that, unlike other superpowers, does not require being bitten by radioactive arthropods. Curiosity is yours for the taking and if you have read more than just this paragraph then you're already a long way down the mental equivalent of the couch to 5K. This book is just a starting point; opening it up was the step into the unknown and now that you're well into the labyrinthine library, you can exercise it yourself. Keep exploring and you'll find things that interest you; ask questions, get answers and, in getting answers, find yourself with more questions. The curious life is a heady mixture of perplexity and revelation and, while it's easier, simpler, to stick to the highways of textbooks and qualifications, I invite you to join me on the road less travelled.

The Road Not Taken
Two roads diverged in a yellow wood,
And sorry I could not travel both
And be one traveler, long I stood
And looked down one as far as I could
To where it bent in the undergrowth;

Then took the other, as just as fair,
And having perhaps the better claim,
Because it was grassy and wanted wear;
Though as for that the passing there
Had worn them really about the same,

And both that morning equally lay
In leaves no step had trodden black.
Oh, I kept the first for another day!
Yet knowing how way leads on to way,
I doubted if I should ever come back.

I shall be telling this with a sigh
Somewhere ages and ages hence:
Two roads diverged in a wood, and I—
I took the one less traveled by,
And that has made all the difference.
Robert Frost

A Collection of Poems by Robert Frost (Canterbury Classics)

Appendix
How I delivered the sessions – notes for teachers

Chapter 2: Topology

Mathematics is my subject and my enthusiasm. For those already curious about mathematics, any foray I make will be fascinating for them. For those not already curious, not so much. This is the difficulty I am faced with if I choose my subject. Journeying down a path that is both technical and abstract doesn't naturally draw anyone in who isn't already on that journey. The answer to my difficulty is pretty obvious. It is the approach one should probably be seeking to take whatever the subject matter. Do something practical. Get them to do something practical.

The first activity is for everyone to draw a network and to count the vertices, edges and faces. This always proves more of a challenge than one would hope, with edges being particularly elusive – I therefore recommend small networks with a handful of vertices and large, clear diagrams to help with accurate counting (fortunately, I know that $V - E + F$ will always give 1 so I have a quick check on anyone who makes an error).

There's a table on the whiteboard and each student fills in their line – quickly we then have enough data that students can make conjectures about the patterns they see and hopefully, possibly with some nudging, get to the rule $V - E + F = 1$.

The next step is to move to solid objects and I have a collection of artefacts to share with them – polyhedral dice are a good starting point but I also have a rock I've drawn a network on, some rubber quoits (which have a hole in the middle) and a figure of eight made out of paper (I'm yet to find a satisfactory two-holed object – my search for a two-handled drinking bowl goes on). In groups of six or so they work on their share of these objects with the rule being one person counts and another checks. When they've agreed an answer, they can put it up on the board which I will have wiped clean. It's important to have a column here to identify the object that is being looked at because they don't all give the same answer and we want to be able to look at the pattern.

There's often a moment at this stage where they convince themselves that they must have got it wrong because they 'know' $V - E + F$ should equal 1 and it doesn't. I encourage them to be confident that they've counted carefully and had it checked and then to put it on the board. 'Perhaps you've disproved maths' is a phrase that can be encouraging – even if they recognise that they're unlikely to have done anything so dangerous.

With a new set of data we can look at the numbers and see what we notice – there are some fairly obvious points here (the numbers are all now even, all the dice have $V - E + F = 2$ ...) so it's a good opportunity to call on quiet or reluctant members of the class to contribute. Eventually, they should reach the conclusion based on the number of holes in the object, at which point I confirm the formula, namecheck Euler and look at the clock.

Depending on the time left, there are a number of ways the lesson can tie up at this point. Quite often there is only time for, 'Thank you, well done, see you next week.' If there are just a couple of minutes then there's a good joke about topologists being mathematicians who can't tell the difference between doughnuts and coffee cups (actually that's the joke – 'good' might be generous), but if you have a little longer there's a lot of mathematics that can be indulged. You can go through the induction proof for planar networks (ones on a piece of paper), take a detour into why there are exactly and only five platonic solids, or leap into four dimensions (a four-dimensional cube equivalent, or 'tesseract', has 16 vertices, 32 edges, 24 faces and 8 'cells' (3D face-equivalents)). We might wonder under what circumstances $V - E + F - C$ gives you zero, although we're more likely to get stuck trying to visualise such a shape (and particularly the cells that form it) and so I prefer to try to use the Euler characteristic to count the holes in a t-shirt.

Trying to do this with an actual t-shirt has so far foxed me and so I have a stylised drawing which imagines what a t-shirt would look like if you pulled the hem out and squidged the arms flat (a t-shirt made from rubber would do this really nicely, of course).

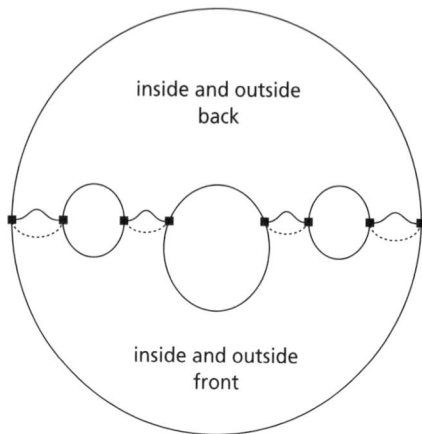

My stylised drawing of a t-shirt

The key point here, and the thing that makes the diagram confusing, is that the t-shirt has an inside and an outside (some people find this a confusing issue with t-shirts full stop) so there are four faces: outside front (the bit with the Van Halen logo), outside back (tour dates), inside back (washing label) and inside front (generally blank). The edges that run along the seams are also either inside (dotted on my drawing) or outside (bold). We therefore have 8 vertices, 4 faces and 16 edges. $V - E + F = -4$ and the t-shirt has three holes. This is not what we think when looking at a t-shirt (it has four: body, head and two arms) but in the diagram and, clearly, topologically, the body hole just becomes the outside edge and there are just three 'real' holes. Which is a point as good as any to leave this curious topic.

Chapter 3: The Palaeolithic era

I start with a page of three questions:

1 Who was the Venus of Hohle Fels?
2 How long ago did humanity start?
3 What is this (together with a picture of an early stone hand axe)?

I then take a 10-million-year timeline and say there are lots of places one might start thinking about how long ago humanity started. I'm going to start with stone tools – 3.3 million years ago – and we can think about at what point these creatures become people. This is where we stop talking about 'creatures' and 'people' and instead use 'hominins' that we may or may not recognise as human depending on exactly what we mean by that word. This is also when we introduce the abbreviations MY (millions of years), kY (thousands of years) and BP (before present).

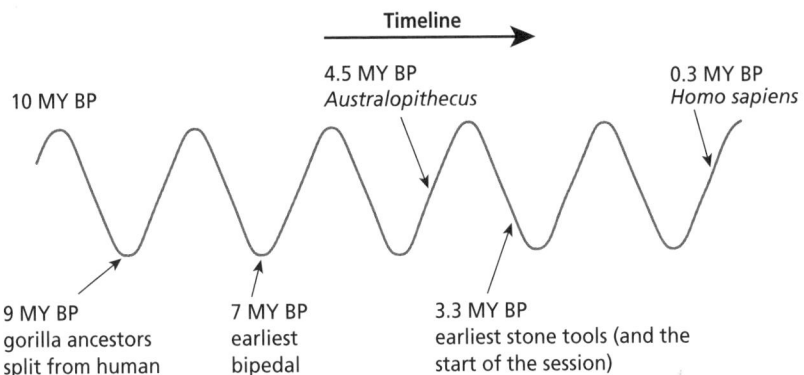

Subsequent slides cover different periods of time with key developments at each point and pictures (typically of a museum's reconstruction of different species – the accuracy of which might leave something to be desired). There is also on each slide a timeline of 3.3 million years marked off in blocks of 50,000 that gets coloured in to mark how far through human history each slide takes us. Technologically, this consists of a table with one column and 66 rows on the right-hand edge of the slide – each slide has more of these cells filled with colour.

Slide 3 (slide 1 being the three questions and slide 2 being the timeline above) covers the time period 3.3 MY BP to 1.6 MY BP. During this time, the hominins are all confined to Africa and we're looking at *Australopithecus* and *Homo habilis*. In this period, we find the first stone tools and can talk about the remains found at Olduvai Gorge. To enliven the slide, we have a museum's impression of *Homo habilis* (the illustration borrowed from the internet) and a small number of bullet points to remind me what I need to cover.

Slide 4 is 1.6 MY BP to 500 kY BP and covers *Homo erectus* and the first expansion out of Africa. The stone tools develop to the rather beautiful Acheulean hand axes and there is fire and cooked food. We have a picture of the Acheulean hand axe and an artist's impression of *Homo erectus*.

Slide 5: 500 kY BP to 300 kY BP. *Homo heidelbergensis* marks the end of the Lower Palaeolithic and we see a northward expansion supported by the first permanent shelters and first clothes. It's possible that this period is also marked by the first language (although we have no idea what that would be like). For some reason, the museum model of *Homo heidelbergensis* has a magnificent moustache – this delights me and some, if not all, of the students.

Slide 6: 300 kY BP to 100 kY BP marks the period when *Homo sapiens* evolved and was confined to Africa while Neanderthals lived in Europe and West Asia. We can track the different genetic groups via mitochondrial DNA and see the flexibility of prepared-core tools.

Slide 7: 100 kY BP to 50 kY BP. This is the end of the Middle Palaeolithic, as *Homo sapiens* expands across the globe – by our standards very quickly, leaving Africa about 80 kY BP and getting to Australia and South Asia 65 kY BP, followed by Europe and China 45–50 kY BP. We know that the lifestyle involved fishing and hunting for large game and eating shellfish and we also know that in Europe, *Homo sapiens* lived alongside Neanderthals.

Slide 8 marks the end of our story and covers the years 50 kY BP to 12 kY BP. This is the Upper Palaeolithic (the next period would be the Mesolithic) and humans are living in organised settlements with cave art, sculpture and music. They make tools such as fish hooks, oil lamps, ropes and needles and expand into America about 15 kY BP. The final picture and final activity is the Venus of Hohle Fels – 'What's this?' The process of guessing and discovery is one of the highlights of the session but which inevitably gets squeezed for time – the ideas of art and pornography and relations between the sexes hangs in the air to colour future discussions or to be picked up later.

Chapter 4: British politics 1979–1997

This is another session that is very content-heavy, with 18 years to be covered in a single lesson and little space for interactivity. The hook this time is the personal story: the idea of five-year-old James going off to 'vote'; of the eight-year-old geek revelling in real-time war statistics without really having an idea of what is being counted; of the 17-year-old who was two weeks from being able to vote in a close election. These 'hooks' worked very well in class both in keeping interest and in engendering questions but it is fair to say that what has worked for me will not work for you and of all the sessions in this book, this is the one that will go least well without significant adaptation.

The structure that allows students to keep track of what's going on and to maintain focus is twofold: people and maps. The opening question is, 'Who are these people?' with pictures of James Callaghan, Margaret Thatcher, John Major, Michael Foot, Neil Kinnock and Arthur Scargill – all (apart from Callaghan) very recognisable faces from the newsreels of my youth, but now ancient history. Margaret Thatcher is usually recognised and John Major often haltingly guessed at, but the others are unknown.

The story of each election is told through the issues it was fought on, the map of how the country voted, and the majority that was won.

- 1979: Margaret v. James (this may not have been the key issue for most political commentators, but it was how things worked as I saw it)
- 1983: Falklands and the Alliance
- 1987: Economy and defence
- 1992: An election Kinnock couldn't lose (but did)
- 1997: Things could only get better

In addition to these key points, I take a diversion with the miners' strike and Thatcher's leadership challenge (and have a slide for each one). Martin Bell provides a charming end-point to the story and a non-partisan illustration of the sense of hope that came with the summer of 1997.

Chapter 5: Art appreciation for beginners

The key element to enjoying art history lies, obviously, not in the engaging narrative but in looking at the art. For some people (definitely me, but I think I'm not alone), the narrative is useful for directing the attention, for letting you know what you're looking at and looking for. As always, this session is not aimed at those who already know about the topic – I'm extremely aware that the artists chosen are very mainstream and that anyone who has a significant interest in art will already be familiar with the content I've shared – it's for those who don't, and particularly those who don't think it's something they would be interested in. My experience so far is that my fears of facing a collection of art history grandmothers armed only with eggs have proved groundless – even those Year 12s studying the subject at A-level have tended to find something new (and, of course, as ever, these are the students who are most likely, rather than least likely, to be delighted to spend 40 minutes on the subject).

The slides I use for this session are simply the paintings in as large and high-resolution reproduction as I can find, together with the date and title to come up on a carefully timed click. The first piece is Constable's *Salisbury Cathedral from the Meadows* and we spend a couple of minutes looking at it, trying to pick out interesting features which we then discuss. In the discussion, I try to dissuade the students from looking for symbolism – not because there isn't any (fairly unusually for Constable, this piece is full of symbolic allusion), but because I think that the interest in art is first what is there and only second what was meant by it. Instead, I direct their attention to the clouds, the trees and the water – all of which are typical of Constable's work. I also ask for a time and place of the setting (they tend to guess England with a lot more confidence than they do the early 1800s). We also spend some time talking about the rainbow, although I tend to be more impressed by this than they are.

The second painting is *The Cornfield* and this time the first question I ask is whether they think it's by the same painter or a different one. To collect all their answers simultaneously and force them to engage with the question, I ask them to point to one side of the room if they think it's the same person and to the other if they think we're looking at a new artist. I make a note of one or two people on each side of the divide and ask them to explain their reasoning.

When all the reasoning on both sides has been explored, I reveal that it's Constable again and point out the similarities of the scene (pastoral England) and the techniques, including the clouds, trees and water. I also look at the date and comment that it seems a less sophisticated picture – simpler, with no attempt at conveying anything as tricky as a rainbow. Even great artists develop their skills over time (heavy editorial hinting that they should spend longer over their homework).

The third painting is *Wivenhoe Park* – rather sneaky as the painting is not really in Constable's mature style (although it's still a peaceful English rural scene with lots of sky and still water). I ask if it's the same painter or a different one and go through the reasoning and then, having revealed we have Constable again, ask if it's earlier than the ones we've seen or later. To my eye it's a simpler composition, flatter, more cartoonish than the others and shows less skill, but I don't always persuade my audience of this reasoning.

Fourth, we have *The Hay Wain* and we have the normal guesses (by now half the class is trying to second-guess whether I'd do exactly the same as I've done the previous three times or if I'm bound to be trying something new). I then explain that this is one of the most popular landscapes in British painting, that it can be seen for free at the National Gallery and, since I have the good fortune of teaching in London, they should go one weekend and see it for real.

We then move onto the Turner paintings, starting with *Calais Pier* which, in some ways, could be a Constable if it weren't for the violence of the sea, the action of the people, the turbulence of the weather – there is a sense of movement even in this very early painting that was absent from the four previous works.

Painting six is *Ulysses Deriding Polyphemus* and the game has now shifted – there are three possibilities: Turner, Constable or someone else (and I think that 'someone else' is a perfectly good shout – I can't really see a good link between this and *Calais Pier* although, as we know, Turner does like a good boat). If there's time, I'll tell the legend of Ulysses and Polyphemus – if not, then we admire the sunset (or possibly sunrise, I don't think there's any way of telling which from the painting) and move on.

Painting seven is *The Fighting Temeraire* and there's a lot to talk about here, starting with who painted it but moving into recognising that it's a painting of two ships rather than just one, explaining that this is the final journey and reflecting on the metaphor that means that the low sun simply has to be setting on a glorious past.

By now I'm inevitably running out of time and so, possibly appropriately, we have a lightning fast glimpse of *Rain, Steam, and Speed* – I wave my hands a lot and talk about the difference between Constable's perfect depiction of the countryside as it is and Turner's attempt to paint the unpaintable, to give the impression of speed on a still canvas.

Chapter 6: *The Second Coming* by W.B. Yeats

You don't have to learn the poem by heart, but if you do then you will have the class' full attention. Suddenly it is not a class, it is theatre – both a delight and a challenge for those of us accustomed to more prosaic subjects. There are very few slides for this session but I do start with one asking, 'What is *Spiritus Mundi*?' and which includes two pictures, one of Yeats and one of the Church of the Nativity in Bethlehem.

I then give students the text of the poem and invite them to read it through and ask for definitions of any words they don't understand. This is quite a good measure of how comfortable they are with the environment – there are obviously words there that are not understood but they're not always willing to admit to it just yet (part of curiosity is a willingness to accept that there are more things to learn – a sense that it's wrong to admit ignorance is one of the things we're trying to overcome). Once we've covered 'gyre', 'falconer', '*Spiritus Mundi*' and anything else that gets brought up, we read the poem round the room, each person reading up until the next piece of punctuation. This is a trick given to me by the aforementioned English teacher that means that they are paying more attention to what is written than the way it appears on the page (the line breaks) – it also conveniently splits up the poem into small enough chunks that they each get a turn.

Once we've read through the text, I ask if there are any phrases they are especially interested in, whether it's because they think the words are particularly striking, or because of the idea conveyed, or because they're not sure what is being said. Hopefully, by this stage in the course, there are enough students willing to air their views that we are able to spend the rest of the lesson going through their suggestions, possibly interspersed with the three questions we started with: what (is *Spiritus Mundi*), who (is this bespectacled chap) and where (is this building)?

There's a lot in the poem to get one's teeth into and the starting point is, in my idiom, what is actually written. Before we can think about the metaphorical meaning of the poem – the political point that Yeats may have been trying to make – we have to understand the imagery of the falcon, the blood-dimmed tide, the stony shape in the desert and the religious significance of 'The Second Coming' and Bethlehem.

When this comes after the British politics session, there's a nice election map that compares the Irish constituencies in the 1910 election (in which the seats were split between the All-for-Ireland League and the Irish Parliamentary Party, both of which were centrist and in favour of Home Rule) with the constituencies in the 1918 election, when Sinn Féin came from nowhere to sweep 73 out of the 105 Irish seats. Sinn Féin was left of centre, in favour of Irish independence (one step beyond Home Rule), and its members refused to take up seats in Westminster, instead creating an independent Irish parliament.

There is also more modern politics as a lens to view this through – starting with the significance of 2016 as a year in which the poem was quoted heavily online (as Donald Trump began his first term) and reflecting on whether the centre of democratic politics will hold, whether it is good for it to hold and what, actually, we mean by 'centre'. In fact, I write this, in the spring of 2025, at the beginning of what looks like a trade war as Donald Trump's second term gets underway, and in a world uprooted from whatever constants had held it secure over the last 80 years. I really have no idea of the conditions under which you might be reading – maybe we'll all get lucky and find someone has answers that don't involve the destruction of civilisation, in which case you'll be able to reflect on what Yeats had to say about stormier times.

Chapter 7: Quantum chromodynamics

Like the topology chapter, this one gets rather technical, but unlike our earlier venture into STEM, there's no physical activity in which to ground the ideas. There are therefore diagrams (I seriously considered putting together animations for this one, but I've never been convinced that they are worth the effort and don't really have the required skills). Fortunately, the colours are useful visually (although the flavours are much less sensually appealing – I'm currently petitioning for a chocolatey quark) and, for those who have a good understanding of GCSE optics, provide an intuitive explanation (intuitive because this is all actually happening on far too small a scale for colours to exist – a quark no more looks 'green' than it tastes of 'up').

I start the lesson with a picture of the solar system model of an atom and ask, 'What is the problem with this?' Then, as my hook for the session, which I hope creates enough intrigue to persuade the non-scientists to get on board, I introduce them to the subatomic octopus and ask, 'What on earth has this got to do with it?'

At some point, when the group is flagging, I will explain that the key question here is, 'How does an oxygen nucleus (with eight protons) hold together?' Eight positive charges should be repelling each other and yet oxygen is stable enough for us to breathe. Either, I say, there is a force acting inside the nucleus that we don't know about or (and I'm not yet prepared to rule this out) there is an octopus, holding the protons together as though they were the north poles of eight magnets. There are, I say, two schools of thought – all the other physicists in the world think it's the first option, but I'm sticking to the cephalopod. The rest of the session focuses on the orthodox line of thought. The third question is, 'What is the colour of the inside of a proton?', to which the answer, eventually, is 'white', but also, 'It doesn't have a colour; the question doesn't make any sense.'

We start with the first question and think about what they've already learned – what critiques of the solar system model do they know? Generally, they haven't even begun to think about the issues of nuclear forces and when they first do, their response is either to hope that the neutrons are negative (which is a common misconception that it's important to clear up) or that the electrons somehow provide the balancing attractive force (which they can't, as that would pull protons away from the centre, not towards it).

We therefore deduce the existence of a force we don't know about. (I've found that some students will have heard about the strong and weak nuclear forces but even then they don't know how they work.) At this point, we have to understand the basics of subatomic physics and, particularly, the mass–energy equivalence that allows you to borrow particle/antiparticle pairs out of nowhere. This is a challenging idea for students who have had it drummed into them that neither energy nor mass can be created or destroyed – I explain that Einstein's equation really tells us that energy equals mass and that we need to believe him. (How could you disbelieve anyone with hair like that?)

The other key idea that needs to be conveyed is that only particles whose colours sum to white can be removed from a nucleon (proton/neutron). I don't use this diagram to remind the students of what I mean by sum to white, but perhaps I should:

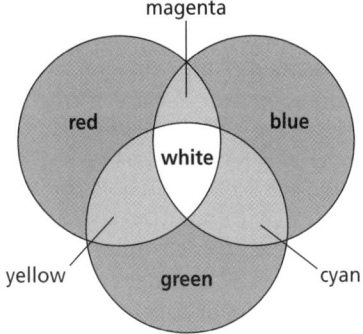

Combining the primary colours of light

An interesting aside here is the reason only 'white' particles can exist in the wild (rather than inside a proton, neutron, meson or other subatomic sanctuary): the strong nuclear force is too strong. The energy required to oppose it is less than that which would make an entirely new proton (using $E = mc^2$) – trying to pull a proton apart simply creates another proton.

Once the 'basics' are grasped, we can go through the force within a proton (which introduces the two-tone gluon and doesn't require any mass–energy conversion) and then the force between two protons (or between a neutron and a proton or between two neutrons, the diagrams are all very similar, differing only in the flavours of the quarks – up or down), using a meson as an intermediary. If there is any time left there is an opportunity to leap into a deeper understanding of nuclear structure and to lay the breadcrumbs for the weak nuclear force but, as with many of these sessions, I'm always running tight to time by the end of the session and dismiss them better informed, possibly bewildered, and definitely a bit more confident to ask questions about nuclear physics. And, almost always, more curious – the answers to today's questions were certainly wilder than we could have hoped.

Chapter 8: American politics, history and government

As you might imagine, there is more here than can be covered in one session and when I decide to run it, I select content depending on the political needs of the moment. In the run-up to a US election, I've looked at the electoral maps of the last few elections and spoken about the process; earlier in the cycle I've focused on the constitutional differences between the UK and the US (particularly if the class has been interested in the UK politics session); and at other times I've indulged myself with the historical development both of the USA and its democracy, with vignettes from particularly interesting elections along the way.

The key idea to get over is that the American system is quite different from the British one – it isn't just a case of translating 'constituencies' into 'districts' and replacing 'prime minister' with 'president': it's better to start from scratch – and the scratch at the heart of American democracy is the series of compromises that allowed it to coalesce into a single country despite quite different lifestyles and world views.

Beyond this, the basic points are:

- There are three sets of elections: the House of Representatives every two years, the president every four years and the Senate, one-third of which is elected every two years.
- The members of the House of Representatives (Congressmen and -women) are based on population – populous states have more members than smaller ones.
- The members of the Senate (senators) are based on states – each state has two.
- The president is voted for by an Electoral College where each state has a number of votes based on the senators plus representatives, and most states are winner-takes-all (the exceptions are Maine and Nebraska, where each district elects one and the state as a whole has just two).

The most important issues politically and socially will be different each time I (or you) run this session – it's one where I reorganise my slides and ideas before I go into it and am keen to get questions from the group. This can make it an interesting departure, moving from lecture format to a seminar/question-and-answer session where students' contributions are as important as my own.

In my slide deck I have pieces of the Constitution so that I can quote exactly, even as I approximate and hedge my explanations; election maps of races gone by with states coloured by party; and sometimes graphics from political websites that are trying to explain or predict the current race (the demise of 538.com is a sad loss for me on this front).

Bibliography

Nowadays, the intrepid champion of curiosity needs little more than an internet connection to lose themselves in the rabbit warren of Wikipedia (which I hold is, along with the Paralympics and the polio vaccine, one of mankind's three greatest achievements of the last century). This modern marvel has, indeed, been my go-to source for specific details that I've needed to track down and serves to bring joy and inspiration when such things are lacking in my life. There are, however, times when only books will serve and I've tried to put together a collection of leaping-off points for further reading from each chapter, gathering together sources I've quoted from, those that I know have informed my understanding and some that I just think you'll find interesting.

Introduction

Bennett, A. (2017) *The History Boys*. London: Faber.

Carroll, L. (2008) *Alice's Adventures in Wonderland*. London: Puffin Classics.

Harari, Y.N. (2015) *Sapiens: A Brief History of Humankind*. London: Vintage.

James, D. and Warwick, I. (eds) (2017) *World Class: Tackling the Ten Biggest Challenges Facing Schools Today*. Abingdon, Oxfordshire: Routledge.

Jonson, B. (1998) *Every Man in His Humour*. London: Bloomsbury.

Shakespeare, W. (2015) *Much Ado About Nothing*. London: Penguin.

Chapter 1

Beckett, S. (2010) *Waiting for Godot*. London: Faber.

Handscombe, J. (2021) *A School Built on Ethos: Ideas, assemblies and hard-won wisdom*. Carmarthen: Crown House Publishing.

Shakespeare, W. (2015) *As You Like It*. London: Penguin.

Stoppard, T. (1980) *Dogg's Hamlet, Cahoot's Macbeth*. London: Faber.

Chapter 2

Crawford, J., Wyatt, J., Schwalb, R.J. and Cordell, B.R. (2014) *Dungeons and Dragons Player's Handbook*. Washington: Wizards of the Coast Publishing.

Ellenberg, J. (2021) *Shape: The Hidden Geometry of Absolutely Everything*. London: Allen Lane.

Steinberg, J. (2015) *Why Switzerland?* 3rd Edition. Cambridge: Cambridge University Press.

Stewart, I. (2001) *Flatterland*. London: Macmillan.

Sutherland, W.A. (2009) *Introduction to Metric and Topological Spaces*, 2nd Edition. Oxford: Oxford University Press.

Chapter 3

MacGregor, N. (2012) *A History of the World in 100 Objects*. London: Penguin.

Roberts, A. (2015) *The Incredible Unlikeliness of Being*. London: Quercus.

Rutherford, A. (2017) *A Brief History of Everyone Who Ever Lived*. London: Weidenfeld & Nicolson.

Rutherford, A. (2019) *The Book of Humans*. London: Weidenfeld & Nicolson.

Chapter 4

Blake, R. (2010) *The Conservative Party from Peel to Major*. London: Faber.

Clarke, C., James, T.S., Bale, T. and Diamond, P. (eds) (2015) *British Conservative Leaders*. London: Biteback Publishing.

Thomas, G. (1985) *Mr Speaker: The Memoirs of Viscount Tonypandy*. London: Century.

Chapter 5

Homer (2006) *The Odyssey*. tr. Fagles, R. London: Penguin.

Honour, H. and Fleming, J. (2009) *A World History of Art*, 7th Edition. London: Laurence King Publishing.

Plumly, S. (2018) *Elegy Landscapes: Constable and Turner and the Intimate Sublime*. New York: W.W. Norton and Company.

Shelley, M. (2003) *Frankenstein*. London: Penguin.

Virgil (2003) *The Aeneid*. tr. West, D. London: Penguin.

Chapter 6

Achebe, C. (2001) *Things Fall Apart*. London: Penguin.

Black, I. (2017) *Enemies and Neighbours: Arabs and Jews in Palestine and Israel, 1917–2017*. London: Penguin.

Cooper, J. (2007) *Rivals*. London: Penguin.

Larkin, P. (2011) *The Less Deceived*. London: Faber.

Shelley, P.B. (2017) *Rosalind and Helen: A Modern Eclogue: With Other Poems*. Norderstedt, Germany: Hanse Books.

Willans, G. (2009) *How to be Topp*. London: Penguin.

Yeats, W.B. (1920) *Michael Robartes and the Dancer*. Dublin: The Cuala Press.

Chapter 7

Cox, B. and Forshaw, J. (2012) *The Quantum Universe: Everything That Can Happen Does Happen*. London: Penguin.

Feynman, R., Sands, M. and Leighton, R.B. (2010) *The Feynman Lectures on Physics*. New York: Basic Books.

Gribbin, J. (2025) *In Search of Schrödinger's Cat: Quantum Physics and Reality*. London: Penguin.

Orzel, C. (2010) *How to Teach Quantum Physics to Your Dog*. New York: Scribner.

Chapter 8

Congressional Research Service. 'Constitution of the United States: Analysis and Interpretation' [Online]. Available at: https://constitution.congress.gov (Accessed: 9 May 2025).

Library of Congress. 'Federalist Papers: Primary Documents in American History' [Online]. Available at: https://guides.loc.gov/federalist-papers/full-text (Accessed: 9 May 2025).

Miranda, L. (2015) *Hamilton* [stage musical].

Chapter 9

Garfield, S. (2012) *On the Map: Why the World Looks the Way it Does*. London: Profile Books.

Rushdie, S. (2008) *Midnight's Children*. London: Vintage.

Tolkien, J.R.R. (2022) *The Lord of the Rings*. London: HarperCollins.

Webster, B.L. and Murdin, P. (1972) 'Cygnus X-1 – A Spectroscopic Binary with a Heavy Companion?' *Nature*. 235: pp. 37–38.

Wikipedia. (2025) 'Bangladesh Liberation War' [Online]. Available at: https://en.wikipedia.org/wiki/Bangladesh_Liberation_War (Accessed: 11 June 2025).

Wikipedia. (2025) 'Partition of India' [Online]. Available at: https://en.wikipedia.org/wiki/Partition_of_India (Accessed: 11 June 2025).

Chapter 10

Anand, A. (2019) *The Patient Assassin*. London: Simon and Schuster.

Wikipedia. (2025) 'Jallianwala Bagh massacre' [Online]. Available at: https://en.wikipedia.org/wiki/Jallianwala_Bagh_massacre (Accessed: 20 May 2025).

Yeats, W.B. (2023) *The Tower*. London: Renard Press.

Chapter 11

Barnes, J. (2009) *A History of the World in 10½ Chapters*. London: Vintage.

Coolidge, S. (2017) *What Katy Did at School*. London: Virago Books.

Frost, R. (2019) *A Collection of Poems by Robert Frost*. San Diego, California: Canterbury Classics.

García Márquez, G. (2007) *Love in the Time of Cholera*. London: Penguin.

Joyce, J. (2000) *Dubliners*. London: Penguin.

de Saint-Exupéry, A. (2000) *The Little Prince*. San Diego, California: Harcourt.

Smullyan, R.M. (2011) *What is the Name of This Book? The Riddle of Dracula and Other Logical Puzzles*. New York: Dover Publications.